# Safeguarding and Protecting Children:
# A Guide for Sportspeople

ISBN: 978-1-909012-38-7

First and second editions
Developed from an original text by Maureen Crouch (NSPCC) in conjunction with the Royal Yachting Association (RYA) and edited by Penny Crisfield (NCF).

Third edition
Author: Gil Lester

The publishers would like to thank the following for their valuable input to the third edition: Steve Boocock, Tim Gardner, Andy Rangecroft, Biddy Rowe and Hamish Telfer.

Fourth edition
Revised by Nick Slinn

Grateful thanks to Vicky Bailey, Carole Billington-Wood, Simon Jones, Kathleen McInulty, Steve McQuaid, Heather Moir, Iain Moir, Paul Stephenson, Anne Tiivas, Matthew Williams and Steve Woolland.

Fifth edition
Authors: Jude Toasland and David Turner

With support from John Mills, Helen Murdock and Anne Tiivas

Sixth edition
Authors: Carole Billington-Wood, Nick Slinn and Dave Turner
Coachwise editorial and design team: Christopher Stanners and Saima Nazir
Cover photo © wavebreakmedia/Shutterstock.com
All other photos © Coachwise/SWpix unless otherwise stated

Published on behalf of
sports coach UK by

sports coach UK
Chelsea Close
Off Amberley Road
Armley
Leeds LS12 4HP
Tel: 0113-274 4802 Fax: 0113-231 9606
Email: coaching@sportscoachuk.org
Website: www.sportscoachuk.org
Patron: HRH The Princess Royal

Coachwise Ltd
Chelsea Close
Off Amberley Road
Armley
Leeds LS12 4HP
Tel: 0113-231 1310
Fax: 0113-231 9606
Email: enquiries@coachwise.ltd.uk
Website: www.coachwise.ltd.uk

Woodland
CARBON
www.woodlandcarbon.co.uk
16069900369
Printed on Carbon Captured paper
Coachwise Ltd

92172

Across the UK, millions of children are involved in a wide range of sports activities, from community participation to national and international level, as athletes, coaches, officials and volunteers. Sport contributes to the overall well-being of children and young people. It is uniquely placed to contribute to keeping children safe and to identify children who may be at risk of abuse in their families or communities.

In 2015, approximately 57,400 children in the UK were known to be at risk of abuse[1]. Research indicates that abuse is significantly under-reported and under-registered, and the unofficial estimate of children in need of protection is many thousands more. Children may be abused regardless of their age, race, gender, culture, religious belief, disability or sexual identity. They are usually abused by people they know and trust, from inside or outside their family. Abusers may be adults or other young people.

Research demonstrates that while participating in organised sport is a positive experience for most children and young people, there was a significant level of abuse reported within sport[2,2a]. In particular, respondents reported concerning levels of physical, sexual and emotional abuse within sport, with a tendency for some groups (eg disabled, talented and LGBT young athletes) to be particularly vulnerable to all forms of harm. However, the Child Protection in Sport Unit (CPSU) has also found that a large number of cases currently dealt with by governing bodies of sport concern abuse identified by the sport but committed by those outside of it. As safeguards are put in place within organisations, there can be an increase in reports as both children and adults become aware of how to report concerns and everyone has the confidence to raise concerns. With a growing number of reported cases of abuse in sport, it is important that every possible measure is taken to ensure sport offers a safe experience for children and that robust structures and procedures are in place to manage the increased number of concerns reported.

People who work with children in sport on a regular basis may be able to provide an important link in identifying a child who has been, or is at risk of being, harmed and in preventing children being harmed, by ensuring safeguards are complied with. Therefore, all those directly or indirectly involved with children's sport have a responsibility to:

- review their own practice in sport situations to ensure it complies with advocated and recognised codes of practice

- identify their values and feelings in relation to child abuse and recognise how these might potentially impact on their responses

- be able to recognise indicators of child abuse and understand the impact of abuse on children

- respond in an appropriate way to children who disclose that they are being abused

- take appropriate action if concerns are raised that suggest a child is being abused.

A number of enquiry reports into the deaths of children in the UK (eg Victoria Climbié in 2000, Peter Connelly in 2007 and Child T[3] in 2016) have highlighted shortcomings in the way a wide range of agencies and services worked together to protect vulnerable children. In response, legislation, strategies and guidance have been developed to ensure children's needs are met both by organisations and individuals that work for them. Their aims are to create a safe environment in which all children can fulfil their potential, and to ensure that those in contact with them are aware of their responsibilities to promote children's welfare. The sport sector clearly has a significant role to play in meeting these aims.

*Working Together to Safeguard Children: A guide to inter-agency working to safeguard and promote the welfare of children*[4] outlines organisational responsibilities to safeguard children, which are outlined in the diagram overleaf.

---

[1] The NSPCC website provides statistical information about child abuse and advice on child protection: www.nspcc.org.uk/statistics

[2] Alexander, K., Stafford, A. and Lewis, R. (2011) *The Experiences of Children Participating in Organised Sport in the UK*. Edinburgh: The University of Edinburgh/NSPCC Centre for UK-wide Learning in Child Protection. ISBN: 978-1-908055-04-0.

[2a] Vertommen, T., Tolleneer, J., Maebe, G. and De Martelaer, K. (2014) Preventing Sexual Abuse and Transgressive Behaviour in Flemish Sport.

[3] In 2000, Victoria Climbié died as a result of abuse by her guardians. In 2007, Peter Connelly (originally, and often still, referred to as Baby P or Baby Peter), a 17-month-old toddler, died after suffering extensive internal and external injuries. Fifteen-year-old Child T committed suicide in Greenwich in 2013, having disclosed self-harm, and experienced domestic violence and abuse.

[4] Department for Education (DfE) (2015) *Working Together to Safeguard Children: A guide to inter-agency working to safeguard and promote the welfare of children*. London: DfE. Available via www.sportscoachuk.org/inter-agency

**All organisations providing services for children, parents or families, or working with children, should have in place:**

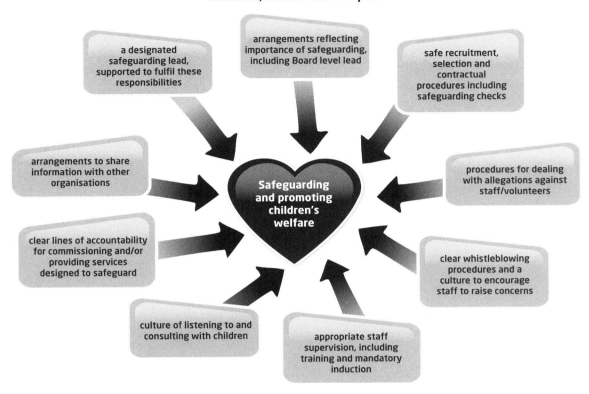

Figure 1: Organisational responsibilities
(adapted from DfE, 2015, Section 2.4)

Further information about the strategies, legislation and guidance in place or being developed in England, Northern Ireland, Scotland and Wales can be found in Appendix C and on the CPSU[5] and government websites[6].

Many governing bodies of sport and county sports partnerships (CSPs) already have safeguarding or child protection policies and procedures. Policies and procedures will apply throughout the sport or organisation, through to club or activity delivery level. All local authority services will be working to a local authority safeguarding policy, which may be linked to that of another department, such as education or social care.

This resource will identify some of the ways your club or organisation is, or should be, operating in line with these procedures. For example, there should be:

- an open and consistent process for vetting and recruiting staff or volunteers whose roles include contact with, or responsibility for, children or young people

- identified club or organisation welfare/safeguarding officers with a clear role description

- codes of practice for coaches, officials, participants and parents

- systems to deal with unacceptable behaviour

- clear reporting procedures, should concerns about poor practice or possible abuse arise (whether inside or outside the club environment)

- guidance on photography, social media, transporting children and away trips.

A number of these issues are considered in greater detail later in this resource.

Support to develop and implement club/organisational safeguarding and child protection policies and procedures can be accessed from the relevant governing body of sport, the CPSU or CHILDREN 1ST in Scotland (details on page 83). In addition, it is a requirement for many club accreditation schemes, such as Clubmark (a Sport England club kitemarking scheme to ensure sports clubs offer a high quality experience for children), in England and Northern Ireland to have safeguarding procedures in place.

This resource and the workshop it supports have been developed and updated to reflect current government legislation and guidance.

sports coach UK is committed to raising awareness of, and implementing action plans for, safeguarding and child protection in sport. sports coach UK is part of a sector-wide safeguarding strategy to establish, maintain and embed safeguards throughout sport. This ensures that sports coach UK is able to provide coaches with the most up to date information on safeguarding and child protection in sport.

Where there are differences in legislation and guidance across the UK, these are referenced in the resource. For further information, contact the CPSU (England, Wales and Northern Ireland) or CHILDREN 1ST (Scotland).

The emphasis of *Safeguarding and Protecting Children: A Guide for Sportspeople* is on safeguarding practice for coaches of children. However, the resource is aimed at all those with responsibility for the organisation of children's sport and those who lead or deliver children's sport programmes. It is estimated that 85% of people undertaking roles such as coaches, leaders, teachers, instructors, development officers, officials and administrators do so on a voluntary basis. The resource contains principles and practice guidelines that can be applied by everyone who is involved with children in a sport environment, regardless of their specific role or title.

This resource is **not** intended as an expert's comprehensive manual. Instead, it offers a practical guide for all those involved in providing sport for children. It aims to help you to increase your awareness about safeguarding and child protection, to recognise the signs of abuse and poor practice, and subsequently deal sensitively and effectively with any issues that arise. It also prompts you to review your own practice to ensure you provide a positive and enriching experience for the children you work with, and that your behaviour is always beyond reproach.

By the end of this resource, you should be able to:

- identify the basis of good safeguarding practice for coaching
- identify what child abuse and bullying are
- describe the indicators of child abuse
- maintain a child-centred approach
- know what to do in response to your concerns about a child or another adult.

In the context of coaching, *Safeguarding and Protecting Children: A Guide for Sportspeople* will encourage you to consider the issues you may encounter when coaching children and, most importantly, to explore what good coaching practice involves. The resource also supports a three-hour sports coach UK workshop, 'Safeguarding and Protecting Children'[7], which you are strongly recommended to attend. This will help you put the theory behind safeguarding and child protection into practice.

If you have had some training and/or experience in safeguarding or child protection already, possibly in another role or context, this resource will help you reflect more on your responsibilities in sport settings and how you may share your knowledge and experience with others. However, you may have had no previous experience in this area and may want to spend more time on some sections than others, or discuss safeguarding practice with your colleagues.

Although this resource is designed for you to work through on your own or as a follow-up to the accompanying workshop, some of the issues covered may raise strong feelings for you. It might be helpful to identify someone who is also working through the resource with whom you can meet regularly to share your thoughts. Make sure you have a clear agreement about how you will work together. Additionally, if you are unsure about the issues raised, you should make a note and discuss these with relevant staff in your club (eg club welfare officer, lead child protection/ safeguarding officer, director of coaching, line or centre manager) or seek further support from the agencies listed in Section 4.4.

While this resource is specifically focused on safeguarding and protecting children and young people in sport, the principles of best practice should apply to all participants (including adults at risk), who should equally be assured of a safe and enjoyable experience.

[7] For further details, see the sports coach UK website: www.sportscoachuk.org

- The term 'children' is used throughout this resource to refer to children and young people under the age of 18 years[8].

- The term 'parents' is used throughout this resource to represent a person or people with legal parental responsibility for a child or young person.

- In the context of this resource, the term 'governing body of sport' is used to refer to all organisations with responsibility for overseeing the policies and affairs of sport.

- The term 'club' is used throughout this resource to refer to any organised sports group.

- In the context of this resource, the term 'coach' is used to refer to anybody working as a coach, leader, teacher, instructor, development officer, official or administrator.

- Throughout this resource, the pronouns 'he', 'she', 'him', 'her' and so on are interchangeable and intended to be inclusive of both males and females. It is important in sport, as elsewhere, that both genders have equal status and opportunities.

- A 'vulnerable adult' according to *Who Decides?*[9], is 'a person aged 18 years or over who is, or may be, in need of community care services by reason of mental, or other, disability, age or illness, and who is, or may be unable to take care of him or herself, or unable to protect him or herself against significant harm or exploitation'. More recently, the term 'adult at risk' is increasingly used[10].

- The Care Act 2014 defines an adult at risk as someone aged 18 years or over who has needs for care and support, is experiencing or is at risk of abuse or neglect, and as a result of those care and support needs is unable to protect themselves from either the risk of, or experience of, abuse and neglect. This will be the terminology used throughout this publication and associated workshop.

- The term 'children's services' is used throughout the resource and includes children's social care and children's social work services departments.

---

[8] There are several definitions of a 'child' in Scottish legislation. Generally, a child is a person under the age of 16 (Children [Scotland] Act 1995). In some circumstances, however, a child is defined as being under the age of 18 (eg a 16 or 17 year old who is the subject of a supervision requirement through the Children's Hearings System). The Protection of Children (Scotland) Act 2003 also defines a child as being under 18.

[9] Department for Constitutional Affairs (DCA) (1997) *Who Decides?*. London: DCA. ISBN: 0-101380-32-1.

[10] Social Care Institute for Excellence (SCIE) (2011) *Safeguarding Adults at Risk of Harm: A Legal Guide for Practitioners.* London: SCIE. This is also enshrined in legislation in Scotland: the Adult Support and Protection (Scotland) Act 2007, which came into force on 28 October 2008.

## SECTION FOUR – Where Next?     **79**

## SECTION FIVE – Activity Feedback     **85**

## APPENDIX A – Safe Recruitment Guidelines     **97**

## APPENDIX B – National Occupational Standards for Coaching, Teaching and Instructing     **99**

## APPENDIX C – Further Information on National Strategies, Legislation and Guidance     **101**

## APPENDIX D – sports coach UK Code of Practice for Sports Coaches     **114**

## APPENDIX E – Workshop Handouts     **118**

## 1.0 Introduction

Sport can have a very powerful and positive influence on children and young people. It should provide opportunities for both enjoyment and achievement. Through sport, children can develop valuable qualities, such as leadership, confidence and self-esteem. However, these positive outcomes can only be achieved if your club has prioritised safeguarding the welfare of young participants, and if the coaching you provide is of the highest possible standard. It is essential that you understand and act on your responsibilities so children can enjoy sport within a safe and secure environment where they feel protected and empowered to express their opinions. Providing children with positive sporting experiences means they will be more likely to achieve their true potential.

This first section will introduce you to the key principles of good coaching practice and relate these specifically to the context of coaching children. As you work through the section, you may well identify aspects of good practice that you already adopt in your work. You may also encounter other issues that have not occurred to you before, but which you may need to address when coaching children in the future.

By the end of this section, you should be able to describe the:

- key principles of sports coach UK's *Code of Practice for Sports Coaches*

- implications of these principles for:
  - coaching in general
  - your club
  - coaching children.

## 1.1 Code of Practice for Sports Coaches

In any profession or vocation, whether paid or voluntary, there are accepted and established codes of behaviour. For example, doctors and solicitors are required to conform to a professional code of practice. Many

companies and organisations now adopt customer charters to ensure the needs of the customer remain paramount at all times. Such codes exist to safeguard the welfare of the customer and protect the service provider from complaints. Codes of ethics describe the beliefs and values that underpin codes of practice, which describe expected behaviour.

A code of practice is just as necessary in coaching as in any other profession. This was first recognised by the National Coaching Foundation[11] in 1995 with the publication of its *Code of Ethics and Conduct for Sports Coaches*, which was based on an original code drawn up by the British Institute of Sports Coaches. Revised in 2001, this subsequently became sports coach UK's *Code of Practice for Sports Coaches*. The following extract emphasises the need for a code of practice in coaching:

> *Coaching, as an emerging profession, must demonstrate at all levels a high degree of honesty, integrity and competence. The need for coaches to understand and act on their responsibilities is of critical importance to sport, as is the need to protect the key concept of participation for fun and enjoyment as well as achievement. This is implicit within good coaching practice and promotes a professional image of the good practitioner. This code of practice defines all that is best in good coaching practice.*
>
> **Code of Practice for Sports Coaches**

The sports coach UK *Code of Practice for Sports Coaches* has been adopted by a number of governing bodies of sport and educational providers of both academic and vocational sports courses. All sports coach UK members[12] must agree to abide by the code themselves, as well as to promote it to all others involved in coaching.

Many sports clubs have added specific points to their governing body of sport's code of practice to ensure the document is specific to their local coaching environment.

---

[11] Known as sports coach UK since April 2001.

[12] sports coach UK membership provides access to benefits and information for anyone with an interest in sport and coaching, and additional specific benefits for qualified sports coaches. For further details, telephone 0113-290 7612 or visit www.sportscoachuk.org

The code is based around the four key principles described below:

> ### Code of Practice for Sports Coaches – Key Principles
>
> **Rights** – Coaches must respect and champion the rights of every individual to participate in sport.
>
> **Relationships** – Coaches must develop a relationship with athletes (and others) based on openness, honesty, mutual trust and respect.
>
> **Responsibilities: personal standards** – Coaches must demonstrate proper personal behaviour and conduct at all times.
>
> **Responsibilities: professional standards** – To maximise benefits and minimise the risks to athletes, coaches must attain a high level of competence by attaining qualifications and through a commitment to ongoing training that ensures safe and correct practice.

These key principles relate to the relationship between coaches and athletes. They may also apply to relationships with other people, including parents, friends, peers, teachers, medics and the press. This list should be an active one, changing as the coaching process develops and as coaches view each child within their individual sporting environment.

The full text of the code is reproduced in Appendix D.

## 1.2 Implications for Coaching

Section 1.1 introduced you to the four key principles of sports coach UK's *Code of Practice for Sports Coaches*. This section will explore the implications of these principles for coaching.

While the principles affect coaching in general, they are particularly important when coaching children. Children, therefore, feature in some of the scenarios in the activities so you can start to focus on this area of coaching. In the activities, you will be asked to evaluate the actions of coaches in specific scenarios, as well as consider what you would do in certain other situations. As a result, you should begin to think about how to integrate the four key principles into your own coaching practice.

### Rights

In order to respect and champion the rights of every individual to participate in sport, you should:

- provide choices for individual athletes in your sport or activity

- provide an environment in which children are free from fear or harassment

- recognise the rights of young participants to be treated as individuals

- encourage athletes to confer with other coaches or experts if the need arises

- promote the concept of a well-balanced lifestyle for young athletes, both within and outside sport.

The United Nations Convention for the Rights of the Child (UNCRC)[13] was established in 1989 and adopted by governments worldwide. These rights are based on what a child needs to survive, grow, participate and fulfil their potential. They apply equally to every child, regardless of who they are or where they are from.

---

[13] For more information on the UNCRC, see the UNICEF website, which includes a summary of the convention: www.unicef.org/crc

## ACTIVITY 1

The aim of this activity is to focus your thoughts on the rights of children and young people. In each of the scenarios in the table below, the coach seems to have forgotten how to be a professional. Consider how they could have handled the situation better and note your ideas in the right-hand column.

| | Scenario | More Acceptable Solution |
|---|---|---|
| 1 | After a tournament, a coach provides feedback that reduces many of her team members to tears. They were up against some stiff competition and played as well as possible. The other teams all hear what is said and feel embarrassed for them. | |
| 2 | After a close match, Scott is blamed for the team losing. His coach later tells other team members that Scott is fat and should go on a diet. | |
| 3 | Sheena needs to take time out from a busy training schedule to observe a religious festival. Her coach is not pleased and says Sheena will lose her place in the team as a result. Several other team members also have religious festivals to observe, but feel unable to say so. The coach doesn't provide an alternative for the children concerned and says she is not prepared to tolerate those who do not put their training first. | |
| 4 | Claire's mother signs her up for a girls-only swimming class as she doesn't want Claire to take part in a mixed class. However, due to a lack of pool availability, the coach combines the girls-only class with a mixed club-training session. She thinks it will be possible to run both sessions at the same time without the groups getting in each other's way. | |
| 5 | A mother tries to sign up her 10-year-old daughter and nine-year-old son for weekly sessions at her local martial arts club. When providing the children's details she mentions to the instructor that her son has a mild learning disability. The instructor immediately tells her that the club doesn't cater for 'that kind of child' – and that while her daughter would be welcome her son will not be able to register. | |

See page 85 for activity feedback.

Coaches should:

- assist in the creation of an environment where every individual has the opportunity to participate in a sport or activity of their choice
- create and maintain an environment free of fear and harassment
- recognise the rights of all young athletes to be treated as individuals
- recognise the rights of young athletes to confer with other coaches and experts
- promote the concept of a balanced lifestyle, supporting the well-being of the young athletes both in and out of the sport.

Action planning:

- What do you need to take back to your organisation about rights?
- What could be strengthened or done differently?
- Consider your club's code of practice – should anything be added?

## Relationships

As a coach, you must develop relationships with children and others that are based on openness, honesty, mutual trust and respect.

You should always:

- consider your behaviour – do not engage in behaviour that constitutes any form of abuse
- promote the welfare and best interests of the children you coach, even if this means letting another professional take over
- take action if you have a concern about the behaviour of an adult or young person towards a child
- empower children and young people to be responsible for their own decisions
- clarify the nature of the coaching services being offered to children and young people
- ensure the best interests of the children you coach when communicating and cooperating with other organisations and individuals.

You should never:

- engage in sexual intimacy with young people at any time, or under any circumstances, including immediately after the coaching relationship has ended. For young people under 16 years old this is simply illegal. For those aged 16 or 17 years, your position of trust places you in a position of authority, with power over the young people you are coaching. These power dynamics make it inappropriate for sexual relationships between coaches and young people they coach and would be against the coaching Code of Practice.

## ACTIVITY 2

The aim of this activity is to apply the relationship principles described previously to your own coaching environment.
1   Consider each of the aspects of coaching in the left-hand column of the table.
2   How would you approach this in your sport? How does this compare to your organisational code of practice? Note your ideas in the right-hand column.
An example of each aspect is provided in the middle column to help you put it into the context of coaching children.

**Note**: Remember that what constitutes good practice in one sport may be deemed inappropriate in another. You may need to consult with the relevant governing body of sport or seek further clarification from a sport-specific development officer. If necessary, explain how the code of practice or guidelines would vary for different performance levels and in different sports.

| Aspect of Coaching | Example | Code of Practice or Guidelines in Your Sport |
|---|---|---|
| Physical contact | For safety reasons, you may need to lift or support a child as they perform a particular technique – your governing body of sport should be able to provide specific guidelines. | |
| Developmentally appropriate training practices | Your sport may require children to participate in weight-bearing activities – your governing body of sport should be able to provide specific guidelines. | |
| Communication | You should assess the most effective way to communicate with all the children and young people in your care. This is particularly important when coaching very young children, or some disabled young people where communication is a significant issue. | |
| Player welfare | You may need to consider how to address needs arising from a player's disability or medical condition, or issues such as player diet or consumption of alcohol. It is good practice to discuss this sensitively with the child and their parents. You may also have concerns about possible harm to a child from outside the sport. It might be appropriate to discuss this with the child or parents unless this would create further risk to the child. Understand that an elite, talented child or young person remains a child first and foremost and their rights as a child should be the primary concern for coaches. | |
| Coaching services | You could find that a child needs medical treatment after taking part in your training session or to address longer-term issues. It is important to talk to the child and their parents to discuss issues such as recommended sports therapists or training implications. | |

See pages 85–86 for activity feedback.

Coaches:

- must not engage in behaviour that constitutes any form of abuse (physical, sexual, emotional, neglect, bullying)

- should promote the welfare and best interests of their young participants

- must never engage in sexual intimacy with young participants (aged 16 and 17 years) either while coaching them or in the period of time immediately following the end of the coaching relationship

- must take action if they have a concern about the behaviour of an adult towards a child

- should empower young participants to be responsible for their own decisions

- should clarify the nature of the coaching services being offered to young participants

- should communicate and cooperate with other organisations and individuals in the best interests of young participants.

## Responsibilities

As a coach, you are in a position of considerable influence and power – particularly when coaching children. You therefore have a profound responsibility to demonstrate and set high moral and ethical standards throughout your coaching practice. Your key roles are to improve performance and demonstrate proper personal behaviour and conduct at all times.

## ACTIVITY 3

As a coach, you have a responsibility to review and examine your behaviour constantly to ensure it conforms to good practice and cannot be misconstrued.

1 With reference to responsibility and professional standards, jot down the issues you would expect to consider both before and during a session coaching children in the left-hand column of the table below.

2 In the right-hand column, note the action you would take (ie what you would do and/or think about) to ensure good practice.

| Issues to Consider | Action Required |
|---|---|
|  |  |

See page 86 for activity feedback.

Coaches:

- must be fair, honest and considerate to young participants and others in their sport
- should project an image of health, cleanliness and functional efficiency
- must be positive role models for young participants at all times.

Coaches will:

- ensure the environment is as safe as possible, taking into account and minimising possible risks
- promote the execution of safe and correct practice
- be professional and accept responsibility for their actions
- make a commitment to providing a high quality service to their young participants
- actively promote the positive benefits to society of participation in sport, including the positive contribution sport can make to achieving improved outcomes for children and young people
- contribute to the development of coaching as a profession by exchanging knowledge and ideas with others, and by working in partnership with other agencies and professionals
- gain governing body of sport coaching qualifications appropriate to the level at which they coach.

## Summary

Good coaching practice involves:

- promoting safe and correct practice in relation to:
  - people – athletes, staff, volunteers
  - places – training grounds, venues, competition areas
- accepting professional responsibility for your actions
- making a commitment to provide a high quality service
- providing a positive benefit to society through sport
- acknowledging that sport is a developing profession and that it is important to exchange knowledge and best practice
- working towards attaining coaching qualifications at different levels
- improving skills and knowledge through continuous professional development (CPD).

The table opposite lists four key actions, together with examples, that will help to ensure good practice in your coaching.

You may like to share your thoughts and ideas with other professionals, colleagues and friends. The process of providing good practice in coaching is a continually developing one and depends on the cooperation and dedication of others.

**Table 1: Key actions**

| Action | Examples |
| --- | --- |
| Follow governing body of sport/employer guidelines. | • Attend training courses and keep up to date with practice.<br>• Seek relevant information to inform practice.<br>• Keep abreast of new developments.<br>• Maintain a professional level of coaching.<br>• Make use of educational opportunities.<br>• Comply with safeguarding and child protection requirements and procedures. |
| Locate support services in your area. | Contact:<br>• other clubs/coaches<br>• sports development officers<br>• injury/treatment experts<br>• specific experts (eg elite level, disability sport or mental health)<br>• local/national squads<br>• trial organisers<br>• schools. |
| Check your own coaching practice. | Review:<br>• feedback from athletes and parents<br>• appraisals/analysis<br>• mentor system<br>• session planning<br>• workload<br>• home demands<br>• own health/lifestyle. |
| Review the social issues surrounding your sport. | • Source local, regional or national initiatives.<br>• Enquire about methods of fund-raising/grants/Lottery funding.<br>• Reward teams and individuals.<br>• Research training weekends, camps and tours. |

## 1.3 Implications for Your Club

This section outlines measures your club can take to promote the key principles outlined in Sections 1.1 and 1.2, and thus provide a safe sporting environment for children.

### Developing a Code of Practice[14]

Most governing bodies of sport and employing organisations already have codes of practice in place, which all the clubs and organisations affiliated to them would be expected to follow. Implementation of these codes can be integrated into and supported by:

- an accreditation process (such as Clubmark)
- a coach education programme
- a commitment to implement and embed policies and procedures throughout the sport
- recruitment practice that includes accessing central information systems (eg local authorities, governing bodies of sport, criminal records checks).

If you are starting without a governing body or organisational code of practice, use the key principles of sports coach UK's *Code of Practice for Sports Coaches* as the basis for a code of practice for your club:

- Begin with a policy statement that recognises the four key principles that were introduced in Section 1.1.
- Outline the importance of relationships among all those involved in the coaching process and relate these to your club's environment.

- If appropriate, involve others, such as parents, welfare or child protection officers, volunteers, teachers and, for elite young participants, advanced coaches. You should also consult children involved in your sport to seek their views on what is acceptable and what is not. This can be particularly helpful when developing codes of practice to promote an anti-bullying culture.
- Amend and update your code regularly to ensure sport continues to be a safe and fun experience for all those involved.
- Consider developing separate codes of practice for different groups of people (eg players, referees, umpires, parents and supporters).

Complying with codes of practice should be a requirement, and not an option, for individuals in the relevant group. It is important that clubs have, or put in place, a policy and procedure to respond to breaches of their codes of practice. Without this, the management of concerns about an individual's behaviour can become very difficult. Most governing bodies of sport, local authorities and CSPs have introduced complaints and disciplinary procedures to deal with such situations, which should be adopted and operated at all levels of the organisation.

Inevitably, all codes of practice have their limitations – to be effective, the key principles must be acknowledged and adopted by all those involved. The aim of the next activity is to illustrate the importance of ensuring that good practice is embedded within the working practices of your entire club.

[14] Also known as 'code of conduct' in some organisations.

## ACTIVITY 4

In the space below, draw a diagram that identifies all the people within your club who you would need to consult when relating the key code of practice principles (outlined in Section 1.1) to the context of coaching children. It may help to place the child at the centre of your diagram. Then consider everyone who will come into direct or indirect contact with the child.

See page 87 for activity feedback.

## Recruitment, Employment and Deployment of Staff

As part of its approach to safeguarding children, your club should have a robust recruitment and selection policy and procedure. This should ensure all reasonable steps will be taken to prevent unsuitable people from working with children. The checklist below covers the main issues to consider when recruiting staff or volunteers.

### Checklist for the recruitment, employment and deployment of staff and volunteers

### Pre-recruitment

- Define the aims of your club (and, if possible, the particular sports programme you wish to staff).

- Summarise your club's open and positive stance on safeguarding and child protection.

- Formalise your advertising procedure.

- Prepare a role/job description; include roles and responsibilities.

- Write a person specification, outlining what you expect of the individual appointed.

- Prepare an application form, asking applicants to provide the following details:

  - name, address and National Insurance number

  - relevant experience, qualifications and training

  - past career or involvement in sport

  - if the role is eligible for a criminal records check (eg in 'regulated activity')[15], a self-disclosure section to establish details of any criminal record, whether any disciplinary action has been taken against them in relation to working with children, and whether they have been subject to any children's services or police investigations in relation to allegations of child abuse

  - the names of two people (not relatives) willing to provide written references that comment on the applicant's previous experience of, and suitability for, working with children – their previous employer is preferable

  - the applicant's consent to criminal records checks being undertaken, where eligible and/or required by law

  - the applicant's consent to abide by the club's code of practice appropriate to the position sought.

Forms should also state that failure to disclose information or subsequent failure to conform to the code of practice will result in disciplinary action and possible exclusion from the club.

### Interview

It is good practice to conduct a formal interview for roles involving working with children and young people. Ensure it is conducted in accordance with an appropriate interview protocol.

### Checks

- A minimum of two written references should be requested, one of which should be from a previous employer. All references should be followed up and confirmed by telephone.

- If the applicant has qualifications, ask to see appropriate evidence (eg certificates).

- If the applicant has no previous experience of working with children, recommend that they seek appropriate training.

- Some roles will be eligible for enhanced criminal records checks. These are posts in regulated activity or otherwise with substantial contact with, and responsibility for, children and/or vulnerable adults. For these posts, criminal records checks should be conducted through your governing body of sport or employing organisation's procedures. If such procedures are not in place, you can obtain more details from:

  - Disclosure and Barring Service (DBS) (England and Wales)[16]

  - Disclosure Scotland (Scotland)

  - AccessNI (Northern Ireland)

  - Child Protection in Sport Unit.

If an individual is working in regulated activity, the DBS will also check whether they are on its barred list, of individuals barred from working with children and/or vulnerable adults.

---

[15] Eligibility for criminal records checks involve activities (including regulated activity) involving close work with vulnerable groups, including children. The definitions of regulated activities are available on the Home Office website – www.homeoffice.gov.uk – and are based around the frequency and intensity of responsibility for children and young people.

[16] See Appendix A for further details.

## Training

- Ensure all new members of staff receive a formal induction to your club (eg introduction to your facility and basic procedures, such as fire drills, safety and first aid).

- All staff working with children are recommended to receive training in the following areas[17]:
  - safeguarding and child protection awareness
  - first aid
  - working effectively with children
  - child-centred coaching.

It is recommended that staff and volunteers working with deaf and disabled children access appropriate training. It is also essential that staff receive regular follow-up training to ensure that they are kept up to date with current issues.

## Monitoring and appraisal

All staff or volunteers should be given the opportunity to receive feedback (eg at the end of a particular sports programme or at regular intervals during an ongoing programme).

## Complaints

Check that your club has a formal complaints procedure, and be aware of how this works in practice. Ensure any staff or volunteers you are responsible for are aware of this. Also ensure parents and young people know how to make a complaint.

## ACTIVITY 5

Think about safeguarding and child protection in your club. What does your club do well and where do you feel there are areas for further development? Comment below.

[17] sports coach UK offers a wide range of workshops and supporting resources in a variety of coaching-related areas. Visit www.sportscoachuk.org for further details.

© Alan Edwards

## Communication

Good communication is vital to the effective operation of your club in general, but is particularly important in the context of coaching children. Good communication will enable all participants to understand what is considered expected behaviour and how to report concerns. This will result in children feeling safe and protected, parents feeling secure in the knowledge that the club is appropriately safeguarding their children, and coaches being clear about what is expected practice and how to respond to concerns.

Establishing and maintaining effective communication channels in your club could involve:

- publishing a newsletter
- producing brief outlines of key policies for young players and parents
- organising fund-raising activities
- setting up a committee
- establishing a supporters' club

- setting up a lottery fund-raising panel
- establishing and maintaining a link with the local sports development officer
- ensuring that the views of young people influence club developments
- providing a coach education programme
- providing in-house training/development opportunities.

Good communication can also enable managers to identify concerns that could be addressed by a coach education programme or a simple change of coaching focus.

## Examples of Good Practice

The next activity asks you to identify examples of good practice at a fictional sports club. Some of these may already exist in your club; others may be things you hadn't necessarily thought of before.

## ACTIVITY 6

Read through the following scenario. As you do, jot down any examples of good practice that you come across.

A number of improvements have been made to Parkgate Sports Club over the past few months. These include the installation of a free drinking-water fountain, a telephone from which club members can make free local calls, security lighting and the services of a night security agency.

The club committee already runs a number of activity schemes and systematically reviews both the quality and scope of provision. All committee members have attended a range of sports administration courses and support the various activity schemes in their capacity as volunteer coaches. The club was recently awarded Clubmark status. The full-time coaching officer is responsible for planning a programme of activities for the entire summer holiday, which involves ensuring adequate staffing arrangements, and managing the behaviour and standards of the club's coaches.

The next plan of action is to organise a sports play scheme during a school holiday for local children aged 7–14. At the first committee meeting, roles and responsibilities are allocated to committee members in order to recruit staff to provide a range of indoor and outdoor activities.

An advert is subsequently placed in a local newspaper and on local community websites. All applicants are required to complete an application form, attend an interview, supply two references, and agree to a criminal records check being undertaken if they apply to work in regulated activity.

All successful applicants are asked to attend formal induction programmes at the club. They are employed on short-term contracts.

With all staff members and volunteers recruited, children are invited to enrol on the play scheme. All of them are asked to complete appropriate registration documents and attend an orientation session, during which club rules, regulations and the code of practice for staff members and volunteers are explained. Parents are invited to attend at least one orientation session per family of children and meet all club staff. They are encouraged to discuss any specific requirements their child may have (eg as a result of an impairment or disability) and how these will be addressed and managed. The club operates an inclusion policy and does all it can to cater for members' specific needs.

Every day, one of the committee members is on duty and responsible not just for general duties, but also for checking facilities and equipment. During activity sessions, the club is closed to members of the public, with entry via a main reception area. Children also use this system to check in and leave. The club encourages parents or a named person to collect their children at the end of their session. Children are invited to provide feedback (either after a specific session or on a weekly basis) and have access to non-coaching volunteers for queries. All courses are reviewed on a regular basis, in terms of attendance and quality.

See page 88 for activity feedback.

## 1.4 Implications for Coaching Children

It is essential that a culture of honesty, integrity and competence exists in coaching. This means:

- understanding and acting on your responsibilities as a coach

- recognising the need to uphold the key concept of participation for fun and enjoyment, as well as achievement.

> **Remember!**
>
> All staff, including coaches who work independently, should not only be required to sign up to your club's code of practice, but also ensure they demonstrate good practice at all times.

### Acting as a Role Model

Not all children may behave as you would like during your coaching sessions. They can be influenced by the media's portrayal of their professional sports-star heroes. Unfortunately, the media tend to focus on incidents of poor, rather than good, behaviour. However, children are unlikely to understand this and may try to emulate undesirable behaviour they have witnessed in major matches or events. This may result in a conflict between you and the children and, if ignored, could have disastrous consequences.

As a coach, you should always try to be a positive role model for the children you coach. If you act in a responsible manner, they will be encouraged to do so too.

Read through the following scenario:

Your team has reached the final of a local competition. On the day of the match, several supporters turn up to watch so the atmosphere is noisy, and the team members are very excited. You know the referee and instruct your team to play fairly, but hard. You emphasise that the referee is tough and they will have to watch their language, tackles and general behaviour. However, you are very pleased that they have reached this stage in the competition, and find it difficult not to concentrate just on winning. During the first half, the score is even, and the crowd is satisfied with the general play and the referee's decisions. However, late in this half, due to a poor tackle from a member of the other team, your best player has to leave the pitch injured. Soon after this, the other team scores and takes the lead. You see that your players are demoralised, tired and desperate to equalise. It is at this point that you notice the standard of their play deteriorates – you also spot incidents of shirt pulling, late tackles and offensive language.

In the space below, explain what you would do during half-time to refocus your players. What would you say to them?

**See page 88 for activity feedback.**

## Empowering Children

As a coach – particularly of children – you hold a powerful and unique leadership role, often carrying considerable authority and status. This role is frequently accompanied by a closeness and mutual trust usually held only between the parent and child. You often wittingly or unwittingly assume this level of authority and, occasionally, your influence spills over into the child's personal life.

One of the challenges you repeatedly face is to manage this potential power and balance the responsible and safe boundary between coach and child being coached. The challenge to do this is exacerbated by the need for you to build high levels of trust from children – particularly those involved in elite performance – in order to encourage them to optimise their performance and develop the level of commitment required to achieve their potential.

When coaching children, you may start by using your authoritative role to build a strong relationship or bond. This can, and often does, result in you having a very positive influence over the child – sometimes an influence that grows even more powerful than that of the child's parents or schoolteachers. Over time, the all-important trust needed normally develops.

However, with this trust comes increased vulnerability and the potential for you to misuse, or even abuse, your power. This might be the result of thoughtlessness, negligence or, occasionally, ill intent. Even a passive type of abuse of power (eg by questioning a child's loyalty or commitment) may sharpen the child's need for belonging. Over time, this may result in over-conformity, obsessive behaviours and emotional dependency.

Individuals may have very different motives, though. For example to misuse their position of trust and power to engage in inappropriate or illegal sexual activities with young athletes. There have also been examples of coaches using their influence to radicalise young people, and recruit and encourage them into antisocial or terrorist activities.

As you become an important figure for a child, you may need to examine your own coaching behaviour. Likewise, the child may develop an inappropriate attachment to you, based on a misunderstanding or misreading of your relationship. Care should be taken to ensure the relationship is an appropriate and positive one, and not one that could be open to abuse or misinterpretation. In this way, you will help to protect the child and yourself, and provide a positive role model for other coaches and children.

Your role as a coach should be to instil confidence in the children you coach so they are willing to play an active role in the coaching process.

Figure 2 illustrates the constituents of responsible leadership. Try to relate it to your own coaching. How well do you manage your relationships with your own participants?

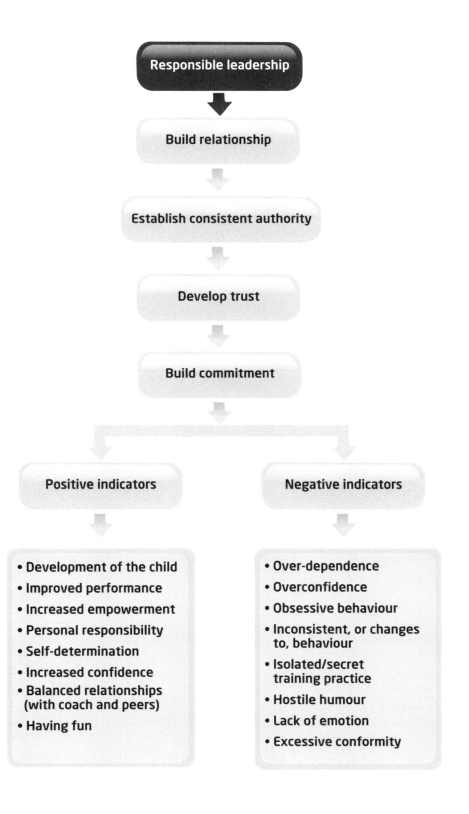

**Figure 2: Responsible leadership**

## Adopting Good Practice

To assist you to become more child-focused and ensure good coaching practice and standards, it is useful to consciously consider how you will meet the needs of the children you coach and respond to the changing coaching environment, the variety of social needs for the children with whom you work, your own skills and expectations, and the demands of others.

### ACTIVITY 8

The good practice toolbox in the left-hand column of the table below contains examples of good practice that you should try to adopt in your coaching practice. In the right-hand column, jot down ways in which you could do this. If you can, add extra examples of good practice in the space provided at the end of the table (on page 21).

| Good Practice Toolbox | Action Points |
|---|---|
| Make sport fun and enjoyable, and promote fair play. | |
| Always give enthusiastic and constructive feedback. | |
| Treat everyone fairly and with respect and dignity. | |
| Build balanced relationships based on mutual trust. | |
| Empower children to make their own decisions. | |
| Be an excellent role model – in your behaviour, attitude and appearance. | |
| Work in an open environment – avoid closed, unobserved situations. | |
| Listen to children and invite their opinion of your coaching. | |
| Communicate with children and parents using appropriate methods, language and terminology. | |
| Understand and address the individual needs of each child in the context of the sport/activity. | |
| Keep up to date with technical skills, insurance and qualifications. | |

| | |
|---|---|
| Observe the relevant governing body of sport's guidelines on contact/manual support of children and explain them to children and their parents. | |
| Involve parents in the supervision of children. | |
| Carry out risk assessments and complete appropriate paperwork. | |
| Keep accurate and up to date records. | |
| Plan ahead for tournaments and competitions. | |
| Ensure adequate staffing for away events in line with club, governing body of sport and local authority guidelines. | |
| Review transport arrangements for staff and participants. | |
| Check all kit and equipment frequently for signs of wear and tear. | |
| Identify when to have a break from coaching responsibilities. | |
| Practise emergency situations (eg fire, injury). | |

**Add any extra examples of good practice that you can think of in the space provided below.**

| |
|---|
| |

## Poor Practice

As well as adopting and promoting good practice, it is also important to recognise and respond to poor practice (ie actions that fail to comply with the key principles of good practice and child protection). These could include:

- encouraging or initiating bullying behaviour
- failing to respond to allegations made by a child
- children using inappropriate language without being challenged
- misuse of electronic communication and social media
- children being reduced to tears as a form of control
- the use of sexually suggestive comments, even in jest
- favouritism of one child
- humiliation of a child in front of their peers

- rough, physical and/or sexually provocative games
- inappropriate touching.

This list is not exhaustive, and you may be able to identify additional examples. In all cases, poor practice must be challenged and attempts made to rectify the situation.

Use team meetings to discuss actual and potential examples of good and poor practice. This will help to foster an open and positive sporting environment.

### Recognising and correcting poor practice

You may think you already have a responsible attitude towards your role as a coach. This may well be the case, but what evidence do you have of this? The following activity asks you to evaluate and reflect on specific coaching scenarios in which you would need to demonstrate responsible and professional practice.

## ACTIVITY 9

Read through each of the following scenarios. In the spaces provided, note down:

a  any views or concerns you may have

b  a possible solution to the situation.

1  A member of your under-15 squad requests individual, one-to-one coaching, even though she is part of a group.

   a   Your views/concerns:

   . . . . . . . . . . . . . . . . . . . . . . . . . . . . . . . . . . . . . . . . . . . . . . . . . . . . . . . . . . . . . . . . . . . . . . . . . . . . . . . . . . . . . . .

   . . . . . . . . . . . . . . . . . . . . . . . . . . . . . . . . . . . . . . . . . . . . . . . . . . . . . . . . . . . . . . . . . . . . . . . . . . . . . . . . . . . . . . .

   . . . . . . . . . . . . . . . . . . . . . . . . . . . . . . . . . . . . . . . . . . . . . . . . . . . . . . . . . . . . . . . . . . . . . . . . . . . . . . . . . . . . . . .

   b   Possible solution:

   . . . . . . . . . . . . . . . . . . . . . . . . . . . . . . . . . . . . . . . . . . . . . . . . . . . . . . . . . . . . . . . . . . . . . . . . . . . . . . . . . . . . . . .

   . . . . . . . . . . . . . . . . . . . . . . . . . . . . . . . . . . . . . . . . . . . . . . . . . . . . . . . . . . . . . . . . . . . . . . . . . . . . . . . . . . . . . . .

   . . . . . . . . . . . . . . . . . . . . . . . . . . . . . . . . . . . . . . . . . . . . . . . . . . . . . . . . . . . . . . . . . . . . . . . . . . . . . . . . . . . . . . .

2 A coach occasionally texts some of the children he coaches. Some of the texts contain jokes about the group he coaches.

   a    Your views/concerns:

       . . . . . . . . . . . . . . . . . . . . . . . . . . . . . . . . . . . . . . . . . . . . . . . . . . . . . . . . . . . . . . . . . . . . . . . . . . . . . . . . . . . . . . . . . . . . . . . . . . . . . . . . . . . . .

       . . . . . . . . . . . . . . . . . . . . . . . . . . . . . . . . . . . . . . . . . . . . . . . . . . . . . . . . . . . . . . . . . . . . . . . . . . . . . . . . . . . . . . . . . . . . . . . . . . . . . . . . . . . . .

       . . . . . . . . . . . . . . . . . . . . . . . . . . . . . . . . . . . . . . . . . . . . . . . . . . . . . . . . . . . . . . . . . . . . . . . . . . . . . . . . . . . . . . . . . . . . . . . . . . . . . . . . . . . . .

   b    Possible solution:

       . . . . . . . . . . . . . . . . . . . . . . . . . . . . . . . . . . . . . . . . . . . . . . . . . . . . . . . . . . . . . . . . . . . . . . . . . . . . . . . . . . . . . . . . . . . . . . . . . . . . . . . . . . . . .

       . . . . . . . . . . . . . . . . . . . . . . . . . . . . . . . . . . . . . . . . . . . . . . . . . . . . . . . . . . . . . . . . . . . . . . . . . . . . . . . . . . . . . . . . . . . . . . . . . . . . . . . . . . . . .

       . . . . . . . . . . . . . . . . . . . . . . . . . . . . . . . . . . . . . . . . . . . . . . . . . . . . . . . . . . . . . . . . . . . . . . . . . . . . . . . . . . . . . . . . . . . . . . . . . . . . . . . . . . . . .

3 You are asked to attend a training weekend where, for supervisory purposes, you are allocated a sleeping area with a group of children.

   a    Your views/concerns:

       . . . . . . . . . . . . . . . . . . . . . . . . . . . . . . . . . . . . . . . . . . . . . . . . . . . . . . . . . . . . . . . . . . . . . . . . . . . . . . . . . . . . . . . . . . . . . . . . . . . . . . . . . . . . .

       . . . . . . . . . . . . . . . . . . . . . . . . . . . . . . . . . . . . . . . . . . . . . . . . . . . . . . . . . . . . . . . . . . . . . . . . . . . . . . . . . . . . . . . . . . . . . . . . . . . . . . . . . . . . .

       . . . . . . . . . . . . . . . . . . . . . . . . . . . . . . . . . . . . . . . . . . . . . . . . . . . . . . . . . . . . . . . . . . . . . . . . . . . . . . . . . . . . . . . . . . . . . . . . . . . . . . . . . . . . .

   b    Possible solution:

       . . . . . . . . . . . . . . . . . . . . . . . . . . . . . . . . . . . . . . . . . . . . . . . . . . . . . . . . . . . . . . . . . . . . . . . . . . . . . . . . . . . . . . . . . . . . . . . . . . . . . . . . . . . . .

       . . . . . . . . . . . . . . . . . . . . . . . . . . . . . . . . . . . . . . . . . . . . . . . . . . . . . . . . . . . . . . . . . . . . . . . . . . . . . . . . . . . . . . . . . . . . . . . . . . . . . . . . . . . . .

       . . . . . . . . . . . . . . . . . . . . . . . . . . . . . . . . . . . . . . . . . . . . . . . . . . . . . . . . . . . . . . . . . . . . . . . . . . . . . . . . . . . . . . . . . . . . . . . . . . . . . . . . . . . . .

4 One of the children at your club is still waiting to be picked up at night from training. There is no one else left at the club, and the child's parents have texted the child to say they are running late. The child asks if you can drive him home.

   a    Your views/concerns:

       . . . . . . . . . . . . . . . . . . . . . . . . . . . . . . . . . . . . . . . . . . . . . . . . . . . . . . . . . . . . . . . . . . . . . . . . . . . . . . . . . . . . . . . . . . . . . . . . . . . . . . . . . . . . .

       . . . . . . . . . . . . . . . . . . . . . . . . . . . . . . . . . . . . . . . . . . . . . . . . . . . . . . . . . . . . . . . . . . . . . . . . . . . . . . . . . . . . . . . . . . . . . . . . . . . . . . . . . . . . .

       . . . . . . . . . . . . . . . . . . . . . . . . . . . . . . . . . . . . . . . . . . . . . . . . . . . . . . . . . . . . . . . . . . . . . . . . . . . . . . . . . . . . . . . . . . . . . . . . . . . . . . . . . . . . .

b    Possible solution:

. . . . . . . . . . . . . . . . . . . . . . . . . . . . . . . . . . . . . . . . . . . . . . . . . . . . . . . . . . . . . . . . . . . . . . . . . . . . . . .

. . . . . . . . . . . . . . . . . . . . . . . . . . . . . . . . . . . . . . . . . . . . . . . . . . . . . . . . . . . . . . . . . . . . . . . . . . . . . . .

. . . . . . . . . . . . . . . . . . . . . . . . . . . . . . . . . . . . . . . . . . . . . . . . . . . . . . . . . . . . . . . . . . . . . . . . . . . . . . .

5   You are asked to coach a child with a disability, but are not given time to discuss her specific personal requirements, either with the young person herself, her parents or her professional carer.

a    Your views/concerns:

. . . . . . . . . . . . . . . . . . . . . . . . . . . . . . . . . . . . . . . . . . . . . . . . . . . . . . . . . . . . . . . . . . . . . . . . . . . . . . .

. . . . . . . . . . . . . . . . . . . . . . . . . . . . . . . . . . . . . . . . . . . . . . . . . . . . . . . . . . . . . . . . . . . . . . . . . . . . . . .

. . . . . . . . . . . . . . . . . . . . . . . . . . . . . . . . . . . . . . . . . . . . . . . . . . . . . . . . . . . . . . . . . . . . . . . . . . . . . . .

b    Possible solution:

. . . . . . . . . . . . . . . . . . . . . . . . . . . . . . . . . . . . . . . . . . . . . . . . . . . . . . . . . . . . . . . . . . . . . . . . . . . . . . .

. . . . . . . . . . . . . . . . . . . . . . . . . . . . . . . . . . . . . . . . . . . . . . . . . . . . . . . . . . . . . . . . . . . . . . . . . . . . . . .

. . . . . . . . . . . . . . . . . . . . . . . . . . . . . . . . . . . . . . . . . . . . . . . . . . . . . . . . . . . . . . . . . . . . . . . . . . . . . . .

6   A child in your care receives a bang to his head. He appears to be fine, and you forget to inform his parents and omit to complete an accident report.

a    Your views/concerns:

. . . . . . . . . . . . . . . . . . . . . . . . . . . . . . . . . . . . . . . . . . . . . . . . . . . . . . . . . . . . . . . . . . . . . . . . . . . . . . .

. . . . . . . . . . . . . . . . . . . . . . . . . . . . . . . . . . . . . . . . . . . . . . . . . . . . . . . . . . . . . . . . . . . . . . . . . . . . . . .

. . . . . . . . . . . . . . . . . . . . . . . . . . . . . . . . . . . . . . . . . . . . . . . . . . . . . . . . . . . . . . . . . . . . . . . . . . . . . . .

b    Possible solution:

. . . . . . . . . . . . . . . . . . . . . . . . . . . . . . . . . . . . . . . . . . . . . . . . . . . . . . . . . . . . . . . . . . . . . . . . . . . . . . .

. . . . . . . . . . . . . . . . . . . . . . . . . . . . . . . . . . . . . . . . . . . . . . . . . . . . . . . . . . . . . . . . . . . . . . . . . . . . . . .

. . . . . . . . . . . . . . . . . . . . . . . . . . . . . . . . . . . . . . . . . . . . . . . . . . . . . . . . . . . . . . . . . . . . . . . . . . . . . . .

7   One of the 16 year olds you coach sends you a friend request to your personal Facebook page and a message asking if you'd like to meet up away from your coaching session.

   a      Your views/concerns:

   . . . . . . . . . . . . . . . . . . . . . . . . . . . . . . . . . . . . . . . . . . . . . . . . . . . . . . . . . . . . . . . . . . . . . . . . . . . . . . . . . . . . . . . . . . . . . . .

   . . . . . . . . . . . . . . . . . . . . . . . . . . . . . . . . . . . . . . . . . . . . . . . . . . . . . . . . . . . . . . . . . . . . . . . . . . . . . . . . . . . . . . . . . . . . . . .

   . . . . . . . . . . . . . . . . . . . . . . . . . . . . . . . . . . . . . . . . . . . . . . . . . . . . . . . . . . . . . . . . . . . . . . . . . . . . . . . . . . . . . . . . . . . . . . .

   b      Possible solution:

   . . . . . . . . . . . . . . . . . . . . . . . . . . . . . . . . . . . . . . . . . . . . . . . . . . . . . . . . . . . . . . . . . . . . . . . . . . . . . . . . . . . . . . . . . . . . . . .

   . . . . . . . . . . . . . . . . . . . . . . . . . . . . . . . . . . . . . . . . . . . . . . . . . . . . . . . . . . . . . . . . . . . . . . . . . . . . . . . . . . . . . . . . . . . . . . .

   . . . . . . . . . . . . . . . . . . . . . . . . . . . . . . . . . . . . . . . . . . . . . . . . . . . . . . . . . . . . . . . . . . . . . . . . . . . . . . . . . . . . . . . . . . . . . . .

8   You are asked to take a squad to an away fixture by yourself.

   a      Your views/concerns:

   . . . . . . . . . . . . . . . . . . . . . . . . . . . . . . . . . . . . . . . . . . . . . . . . . . . . . . . . . . . . . . . . . . . . . . . . . . . . . . . . . . . . . . . . . . . . . . .

   . . . . . . . . . . . . . . . . . . . . . . . . . . . . . . . . . . . . . . . . . . . . . . . . . . . . . . . . . . . . . . . . . . . . . . . . . . . . . . . . . . . . . . . . . . . . . . .

   . . . . . . . . . . . . . . . . . . . . . . . . . . . . . . . . . . . . . . . . . . . . . . . . . . . . . . . . . . . . . . . . . . . . . . . . . . . . . . . . . . . . . . . . . . . . . . .

   b      Possible solution:

   . . . . . . . . . . . . . . . . . . . . . . . . . . . . . . . . . . . . . . . . . . . . . . . . . . . . . . . . . . . . . . . . . . . . . . . . . . . . . . . . . . . . . . . . . . . . . . .

   . . . . . . . . . . . . . . . . . . . . . . . . . . . . . . . . . . . . . . . . . . . . . . . . . . . . . . . . . . . . . . . . . . . . . . . . . . . . . . . . . . . . . . . . . . . . . . .

   . . . . . . . . . . . . . . . . . . . . . . . . . . . . . . . . . . . . . . . . . . . . . . . . . . . . . . . . . . . . . . . . . . . . . . . . . . . . . . . . . . . . . . . . . . . . . . .

See page 88 for activity feedback.

## 1.5 Summary

In this first section, you have been introduced to four key principles relating to good coaching practice:

- rights

- relationships

- responsibilities: personal standards

- responsibilities: professional standards.

You have also considered these principles in the context of coaching children and should now understand the crucial role you play in the development of sport and in the lives of the children you coach.

You should also have begun to think about the issues arising from the key principles and the actions required to address them. Good practice involves ensuring these actions result in a professional approach to coaching where there is evidence of honesty, integrity and competence. The aim is to provide sporting opportunities for children – for fun as well as for achievement – within a safe and secure environment.

For further information relating to some of the issues explored in this section, the sports coach UK *Code of Practice for Sports Coaches* (2010) leaflet[18] is recommended. There are also a number of briefing papers available on the CPSU website and in the CPSU e-newsletter[19].

In the next section, you will start to address the issues surrounding child abuse in general and, in particular, concerns arising in sport. Examine your own feelings as you work through it. Initially, you may believe it has nothing to do with you because you think child abuse does not happen in your sport. Alternatively, you may accept that it occurs, but feel this material is irrelevant because it does not apply to your own behaviour (or that of your peer-group coaches). The material may arouse a strong emotional reaction, perhaps because you have been abused yourself, know someone who has, or have concerns about a particular child or adult with whom you work. Whatever your initial feelings, you will not be alone. You may also find that your attitude or feelings change as you work through the resource.

© wavebreakmedia/Shutterstock.com

---

[18] The code is included in Appendix D. The leaflet is also available from 1st4sport.com (Tel: 0113-201 5555 or visit www.1st4sport.com).

[19] To subscribe to the CPSU e-newsletter, email cpsu@nspcc.org.uk

## 2.0 Introduction

All those directly or indirectly involved with children's sport have a responsibility to:

- be able to recognise and respond to signs of child abuse

- identify their values and feelings in relation to child abuse, and recognise how these may impact on their responses.

Even for those experienced in working with child abuse, it is not always easy to recognise situations where abuse has already taken place or may potentially occur. As a coach, you are not expected to be an expert, but you do have a responsibility to act if you have any concerns about the behaviour of an adult or a child towards another child. In this section, you will be given the opportunity to explore what child abuse is and consider your own feelings, beliefs and values in relation to it. Through the use of case studies, you will begin to understand categories of abuse and then be encouraged to start to recognise the signs of child abuse. Although quite factual, this section is intended to stimulate both thought and discussion. By the end of the section, you should be able to:

- consider your own beliefs and preconceived ideas about child abuse

- describe the different categories of child abuse

- describe the effects of abuse

- describe the incidence of abuse and identify those children most at risk

- identify the signs of child abuse in sports situations.

## 2.1 What Constitutes Child Abuse?

### Abuse and Poor Practice

The term 'child abuse' is used to describe all the ways in which children are harmed, usually by adults and often by those they know and trust. 'Harm' refers to the damage that has been, or may be, done to a child's physical or mental health or development. This may occur at home, at school or in a community setting, including a sport environment. An adult may abuse a child both by inflicting, and by failing to prevent, abuse.

Alternatively, a child may abuse another child – indeed, research tells us that peer abuse in sport is an increasing concern for young people[20]. The extent of emotional abuse has also been highlighted by research, drawing attention to the damage this can cause and how it can create a platform from which other forms of abuse can occur.

Poor practice refers to behaviour, generally by staff and volunteers, that does not comply with the code of practice for the club. If poor practice continues and escalates without being addressed, it can become abusive (eg a coach who fails to understand the needs of young people who they are training and pushes them beyond what is appropriate, or an official who is friends with young players on Facebook against the club's guidance).

All concerns about identified or suspected abuse and poor practice should be reported. Concerns about abuse are likely to be referred to statutory authorities to lead investigations into these. Concerns about poor practice are more likely to be handled in-house either by the club or governing body of sport.

### Child Abuse

Some adults and young people who are motivated to harm children deliberately seek out opportunities to work or volunteer in environments that offer access to young people. This may include education and social care settings (eg schools or residential homes) or other community settings (eg youth or sports clubs). It is therefore important that any organisations or groups that provide services for children and young people have effective recruitment and deployment systems in place. This process is designed to limit access to children and young people by those known or believed to represent a risk to them, and should include seeking appropriate references and criminal records checks (see page 12 and Appendix A).

The next activity is designed to begin to address your own feelings when faced with an incident of potential child abuse.

[20] Alexander, K., Stafford, A. and Lewis, R. (2011) *The Experiences of Children Participating in Organised Sport in the UK*. Edinburgh: The University of Edinburgh/NSPCC Centre for UK-wide Learning in Child Protection. ISBN: 978-1-908055-04-0.

Read through the following scenario:

At the end of a coaching session, you dismiss your group of children and escort them to the changing area. Outside the changing rooms, you notice several parents waiting to collect their children and go across to join them. As the children reappear from the changing rooms, you notice one mum looking cross as her son George trails various items of clothing across the floor, dropping a pile of clothes at her feet. George's mother has parked on a double yellow line and can see a traffic warden approaching. George struggles to put his kit in his bag and can't find one of his trainers. His mother pushes him back quite harshly in the direction of the changing rooms and shouts at him to hurry up. You notice that there are two other children in George's mother's car, both of whom appear to be crying. When George finally emerges from the changing rooms with his missing trainer, his mother is having a lively discussion with the traffic warden who, despite her pleas, gives her a parking ticket. George attempts to get in the car and is roughly pushed in by his mother who continues to shout and blames him for the parking fine. The last you see is George rubbing his head, in tears, as he fumbles with his seat belt.

Now jot down your initial feelings:

**See page 88 for activity feedback.**

Try to identify what you understand by the term 'abuse' by assessing the situations in the following activity.

## ACTIVITY 11

**Remember!**

Defining child abuse is made more difficult because of each person's different values and ideas about what constitutes child abuse. Most of the statements below do not provide enough information for you to determine whether the behaviour constitutes neglect or abuse.

However, as a coach, **it is not your responsibility to decide.** Your role is to be aware of possible signs of abuse in order to inform others appropriately.

Consider which of the following behaviours between children and adults are acceptable and which are not, and identify your reason(s):

1   A four-year-old child is left alone in a supermarket car park while a parent does the weekly shopping.

Not acceptable/acceptable

Reason(s): ....................................................................................................

....................................................................................................

....................................................................................................

2   A 12-year-old child is left alone in the evening to play computer games while his parents go to a restaurant.

Not acceptable/acceptable

Reason(s): ....................................................................................................

....................................................................................................

....................................................................................................

3   A child is late to a training session because she was talking to some friends after her parents dropped her off. As a punishment, the coach asks her to do a small number of press-ups before joining the training group.

Not acceptable/acceptable

Reason(s): ....................................................................................................

....................................................................................................

....................................................................................................

4   A coach tells a child they need to go on a diet if they are to make the team.

Not acceptable/acceptable

Reason(s): ....................................................................................................

....................................................................................................

....................................................................................................

5   A famous sportsperson visits your under-15 team and asks to stay late to hold a private one-to-one coaching session with your most talented child.

Not acceptable/acceptable

Reason(s): ....................................................................................................

........................................................................................................

........................................................................................................

6   A female coach enters the boys' changing room to talk to the players before the competition.

Not acceptable/acceptable

Reason(s): ....................................................................................................

........................................................................................................

........................................................................................................

7   A male coach physically supports a young female gymnast during a tumbling routine.

Not acceptable/acceptable

Reason(s): ....................................................................................................

........................................................................................................

........................................................................................................

8   A coach has sexual intercourse with one of their 16-year-old athletes.

Not acceptable/acceptable

Reason(s): ....................................................................................................

........................................................................................................

........................................................................................................

9   A male coach expresses his delight following a good performance by hugging one of his athletes.

Not acceptable/acceptable

Reason(s): ....................................................................................................

........................................................................................................

........................................................................................................

10  A teacher has sexual intercourse with a 15 year old in their class.

Not acceptable/acceptable

Reason(s): ....................................................................................................

........................................................................................................

........................................................................................................

11  A female coach works alone with a squad of male athletes.

Not acceptable/acceptable

Reason(s): ................................................................................................................

........................................................................................................................

........................................................................................................................

12  After a challenging training session, one eight-year-old child is so tired, they faint.

Not acceptable/acceptable

Reason(s): ................................................................................................................

........................................................................................................................

........................................................................................................................

13  A teammate leaves threatening messages on a child's social networking page after a poor performance.

Not acceptable/acceptable

Reason(s): ................................................................................................................

........................................................................................................................

........................................................................................................................

14  A child joins a club where the 'tradition' is for new members to take part in a humiliating ceremony.

Not acceptable/acceptable

Reason(s): ................................................................................................................

........................................................................................................................

........................................................................................................................

15  A coach is providing videos to members of their club and inviting certain club members to attend political rallies of a group they are a member of. You soon notice a change in the behaviour of some of those who attended.

Not acceptable/acceptable

Reason(s): ................................................................................................................

........................................................................................................................

........................................................................................................................

See pages 88–89 for activity feedback.

## ACTIVITY 11a - Martial Arts Scenarios

1   A four-year-old child is left alone in a supermarket car park while a parent does the weekly shopping.

Not acceptable/acceptable

Reason(s): ...........................................................................................................................

...........................................................................................................................

...........................................................................................................................

2   A 12-year-old child is left alone in the evening to play computer games while his parents go to a restaurant.

Not acceptable/acceptable

Reason(s): ...........................................................................................................................

...........................................................................................................................

...........................................................................................................................

3   A child is late to a class because she was talking to some friends after her parents dropped her off. As a punishment, the instructor asks her to do a small number of press-ups before joining the group.

Not acceptable/acceptable

Reason(s): ...........................................................................................................................

...........................................................................................................................

...........................................................................................................................

4   An instructor tells a child they need to go on a diet if they are to be selected.

Not acceptable/acceptable

Reason(s): ...........................................................................................................................

...........................................................................................................................

...........................................................................................................................

5   A famous martial artist visits your under-15 class and asks to stay late to hold a private one-to-one class with your most talented child.

Not acceptable/acceptable

Reason(s): ...........................................................................................................................

...........................................................................................................................

...........................................................................................................................

6   A female instructor enters the boys' changing room to talk to the students before a grading.

Not acceptable/acceptable

Reason(s): ...................................................................................

.....................................................................................

.....................................................................................

7   A male instructor physically supports a young female student to correct her stance.

Not acceptable/acceptable

Reason(s): ...................................................................................

.....................................................................................

.....................................................................................

8   An instructor has sexual intercourse with one of their 16-year-old students.

Not acceptable/acceptable

Reason(s): ...................................................................................

.....................................................................................

.....................................................................................

9   A male instructor expresses his delight following a good performance by hugging one of his students.

Not acceptable/acceptable

Reason(s): ...................................................................................

.....................................................................................

.....................................................................................

10  A school teacher has sexual intercourse with a 15 year old from their class.

Not acceptable/acceptable

Reason(s): ...................................................................................

.....................................................................................

.....................................................................................

11  A female instructor works alone with a group of male students.

Not acceptable/acceptable

Reason(s): ...................................................................................

.....................................................................................

.....................................................................................

12 After a challenging class, one eight-year-old child is so tired, they faint.

Not acceptable/acceptable

Reason(s): ...............................................................................................................

...............................................................................................................

...............................................................................................................

13 A student leaves threatening messages on a child's social networking page after a poor performance.

Not acceptable/acceptable

Reason(s): ...............................................................................................................

...............................................................................................................

...............................................................................................................

14 A child joins a club where the 'tradition' is for new members to take part in a humiliating ceremony.

Not acceptable/acceptable

Reason(s): ...............................................................................................................

...............................................................................................................

...............................................................................................................

15 An instructor is providing videos to members of their club and inviting certain club members to attend political rallies of a group they are a member of. You soon notice a change in the behaviour of some of those who attended.

Not acceptable/acceptable

Reason(s): ...............................................................................................................

...............................................................................................................

...............................................................................................................

## 2.2 Truths and Myths

Having explored your feelings a little more fully, consider your current knowledge about child abuse by thinking about the questions in the next activity.

### ACTIVITY 12

A number of commonly held views are stated below. Decide whether these views are true or false. Remember that these statements refer to the culture of the UK so your answers should be in that context.

| | | |
|---|---|---|
| 1 | Children are abused mostly by strangers. | True/False |
| 2 | It is only men who sexually abuse children. | True/False |
| 3 | Disabled children are less likely to be victims of abuse. | True/False |
| 4 | Girls are much more likely to be abused than boys. | True/False |
| 5 | In some cultures, it is acceptable for children to be abused. | True/False |
| 6 | If children's services are involved, children are usually removed from their homes. | True/False |
| 7 | Children are resilient and, therefore, recover quickly from abuse. | True/False |
| 8 | Abuse in a sporting context is unlikely. | True/False |
| 9 | Children often go to great lengths to cover up the fact that they are being abused. | True/False |
| 10 | Coaches are the people most likely to abuse a child in sport. | True/False |

**See pages 89–90 for activity feedback.**

Activities 11 and 12 helped you consider some of your own beliefs and preconceived ideas about child abuse. This will help you to remain open-minded and receptive to the following information about categories and signs of abuse.

## 2.3 Categories of Child Abuse

Child abuse can take many forms, but can be broadly separated into five main categories:

* neglect

* physical abuse

* sexual abuse

* emotional abuse

* bullying (although not a category of abuse, bullying incidents can have damaging consequences for children).

Some forms of abuse (including grooming, sexual, emotional abuse and bullying) often take place online, for example through social media.

### Neglect

Neglect occurs when adults fail to meet a child's basic physical and/or psychological needs, and is likely to result in the serious impairment of the child's health or development.

Examples of neglect include:

* failing to provide adequate food, shelter or clothing

* regularly leaving a child alone or unsupervised

* failing to protect a child from physical harm or danger

* failing to ensure access to appropriate medical care or treatment

* refusing to give a child affection and attention.

### Examples in sport

Neglect in a sport situation could include a coach failing to ensure a pitch is suitable to train on, or exposing children to extreme temperatures during a coaching session.

## ACTIVITY 13

In the left-hand column of the table below, list situations in which neglect could occur in your sport. In the right-hand column, identify examples of good practice you undertake to ensure the safety of the children you coach.

| Potential Examples of Neglect | Examples of Good Practice |
|---|---|
|  |  |

## Physical Abuse

Physical abuse occurs when someone causes physical harm or injury to a child.

Examples include:

- hitting, shaking or throwing a child
- poisoning, burning or scalding a child
- biting, suffocating or drowning a child
- giving a child inappropriate drugs or alcohol
- otherwise causing them deliberate physical harm.

## Examples in sport

Physical abuse in a sport situation may be deemed to occur if the nature and intensity of training and competition exceed the capacity of the child's developmental stage. This includes instances where prohibited substances are used to delay puberty, control diet or enhance performance. Another example of physical abuse in sport is a coach physically punishing a child for a performance.

## ACTIVITY 14

Think of concerns about physical issues relating to your sport and the children you coach. How could these be addressed? An example has been given to start you off.

### Example

*Should I encourage children to consume products advertised as high-energy drinks or tablets prior to a competition?*

See page 90 for activity feedback.

## Sexual Abuse

Sexual abuse occurs when adults (both male and female) or other young people use children to meet their own sexual needs. This could include:

- full sexual intercourse

- masturbation, oral sex, anal intercourse or fondling

- involving a child in producing pornographic material (eg videos, photographs)

- showing a child pornographic material (eg magazines, videos, pictures).

### Examples in sport

There are situations within all sports where the potential for this form of abuse exists.

- Some individuals have deliberately targeted sports activities in order to gain access to, and abuse, children.

- There is evidence that individuals have sometimes ignored codes of practice and used physical contact within a coaching role to mask their inappropriate touching of children (eg while supporting an athlete on a piece of equipment).

- Some coaches consider it an acceptable part of the sport's culture to have a sexual relationship with the children they coach.

- Some people have used sporting events as an opportunity to take inappropriate photographs or videos of sportspeople (including young and disabled participants) in vulnerable positions.

- Some people have used involvement in sports clubs as a method of 'grooming' children.

- Increasingly, abusers are using social media to contact and groom young people they have identified through sports activities.

The term 'grooming' refers to the way in which sexual abusers (or potential abusers) manipulate targeted victims, professional carers, colleagues and their environment. They do this to make it easier to abuse children and reduce the likelihood of the child either telling/disclosing or being believed, should they share what is happening.

Grooming behaviours may appear to be positive (eg providing a particular child or group with extra attention/treats/lifts to and from events, or the individual making himself highly thought of and indispensable within a club), and the plausibility of the individuals concerned often makes it difficult for others to identify their real motivation. However, they will also ignore, undermine or resist the application of good practice and other safeguarding guidelines.

Adherence to codes of practice, an understanding of acceptable/unacceptable behaviour, an open culture within the club to challenge poor practice, and an awareness on the part of everyone in a club of when and how to report concerns will all contribute to identifying and dealing with grooming behaviours. Concerns about an adult's behaviour should be reported to the relevant club welfare or safeguarding officer.

## ACTIVITY 15

In the space provided below, record specific guidelines relating to physical contact in your sport. If you are not sure, contact your governing body of sport for advice and guidance.

See page 90 for activity feedback.

## Emotional Abuse

This refers to the emotional ill treatment of a child that results in severe and persistent adverse effects on their emotional development. Although it can occur in isolation, children who have suffered neglect or physical/sexual abuse will also have suffered some level of emotional abuse. Research shows that children who experience an emotionally abusive environment are at higher risk of suffering other forms of abuse. Children of all ages can be emotionally abused in a number of ways, such as through:

• imposing developmentally inappropriate expectations on them

• making them feel worthless, unloved, inadequate or valued only in so far as they meet the needs of another person

• making their positive self-image entirely dependent on sporting achievement and success

• making them feel frightened or in danger

• shouting at, threatening or taunting them

• overprotecting them or, conversely, failing to give them the love and affection they need.

## Examples in sport

Emotional abuse may occur in sport if children are subjected to constant criticism, name-calling, sarcasm, bullying, racism or unrealistic pressure to consistently perform to high expectations. In some cases, this may come from parents and coaches. The inappropriate use or availability of personal information or images (in the media, Internet, photographs or even a club noticeboard) can be distressing for any participant. As a result of emotional abuse, children may feel nervous, lack confidence and self-worth, and learn to dislike any form of activity. It is up to the coach to lead by example and ensure concerning incidents are handled with care and sensitivity so the situation is controlled and not made worse.

In the diagram below, there are various people who could be responsible for subjecting a child to emotional abuse. For each section, give an example of how you could guard against this happening in your sport.

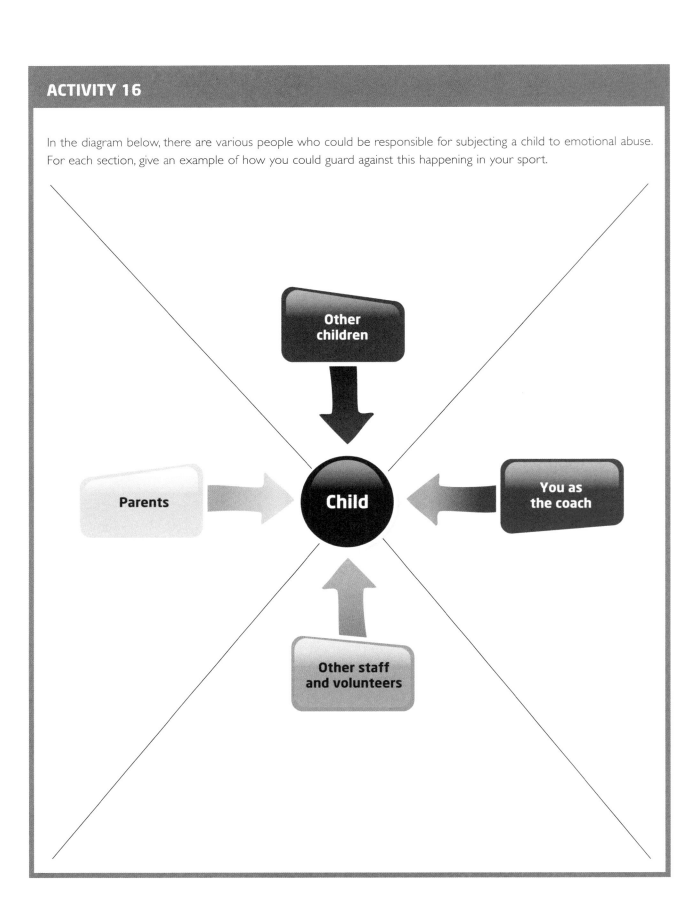

## Bullying

Bullying is deliberately hurtful behaviour, usually repeated over a period of time, where it is difficult for those being bullied to defend themselves. It can be verbal, written or physical and can include actions such as:

- physical assaults
- name-calling, sarcasm and racist taunts
- threats and gestures
- unwanted physical contact
- graffiti
- stealing or hiding personal items
- being ostracised or ignored.

Bullying can also occur via the Internet, through blogging and social networking sites, and by phone, through text messaging.

Each year, over 30,000 children call ChildLine about bullying. Research suggests that almost half (46%) of children and young people said they had been bullied at school at some point in their lives, with 38% of disabled children worried about being bullied[21].

Although anyone can be the target of bullying, victims are typically shy, sensitive or insecure. Sometimes, they are singled out for physical reasons (eg being overweight or smaller than everyone else, having a disability or belonging to a different race, faith or culture) or because of their sports ability or success.

The effects of bullying may be invisible, but can leave lasting emotional scars. The bully is not always obvious to others, and the victim often keeps quiet.

It is estimated that one in three children have been a victim of cyber-bullying[22].

## Examples in sport

The competitive nature of sport makes it an ideal environment for the bully. The bully could be:

- a parent who pushes his child too hard
- a coach who shouts at, or humiliates, children
- a child who actively seeks to make sport a difficult or unhappy experience for others. Although bullying often takes place in schools, it can and does occur wherever there is the opportunity for children to meet (eg changing rooms, practice and social areas in sports centres, during journeys to and from sports activities) or interact (eg social networking environments). The bully may not be selective in the location, but is always likely to be careful about who else may be able to observe what is said or done. The damage inflicted by bullying is frequently underestimated. It can cause considerable distress to some children, to the extent that they may stop participating in sport altogether.

Although it may be difficult for you to anticipate when your actions could provide further opportunities for the bully, you have a responsibility to ensure sport is a positive experience for all children. Carefully observe the children you coach to evaluate whether they are being included in activities by other children and whether they have the confidence to voice any doubts they may have. It is easy to tell if children are unhappy – you cannot get the best out of them if they are hurting emotionally. Many governing bodies of sport now have anti-bullying policies and encourage children, coaches and sometimes parents to sign up to codes of conduct. They may also have specific guidance around use of social networking sites and texting, photography etc in order to ensure all participants and those responsible for them are clear about expectations in these areas.

---

[21] Chamberlain, T., George, N., Golden, S., Walker, F. and Benton, T. (2010) *Tellus4 National Report.* London: DCSF. ISBN: 978-1-847757-19-7.

[22] McAfee (2014) 'Survey of children and parents', *The Guardian,* 14 November 2014.

Read through the following scenarios and consider whether they present any concerns and how you might respond.

| Scenario | Does this present any concerns, and if so, why? How might you respond to this situation? |
|---|---|
| 1 You notice a member of a team that you coach will not get changed at the same time as everyone else. She always arrives in her kit and stays late to clear up the equipment or just to chat so that by the time she goes into the changing rooms, everyone else is leaving. She declines the offer of a free fitness test and fails to attend a club outing to the local swimming pool. When you think about it, you realise that this child always remains fully covered for every activity and is often on her own. | |
| 2 You have a new member of the group in training who is a young woman with Down's syndrome. Her mother has explained that she requires careful explanations of activities. You have a large group to manage already and try to engage this new member as best you can. Some of the other young people are getting frustrated with explaining activities to her. At the end of the session, you find her in tears in a corner, but she will not tell you why. | |
| 3 You ask a group you coach to work with an older team for training purposes. Most of the group members feel that this is an excellent idea, but some look worried. The older team are technically skilled players. They are bigger and heavier, and have a reputation for playing very hard. | |

**See pages 90–91 for activity feedback.**

## 2.4 Effects of Abuse

The experience of abuse can have major long-term effects on all aspects of a child's health, growth, development and well-being, and subsequently affect them into adulthood. This can include a wide range of many complex social and economic problems, with an increased likelihood of mental disorders, health problems, education failure and unemployment, substance addiction, crime and delinquency, homelessness and abusive behaviour towards others.

However, there are vast individual differences in immediate and long-term responses to childhood abuse. Support from within and outside the family, appropriate responses to stop the abuse and address the behaviour of the abuser, and therapeutic work with the child, where helpful, can all enhance the child's resilience and reduce the likelihood of long-term damage.

As a result of abuse, children may:

* die – clearly the most serious effect

* suffer pain and distress

* develop behavioural difficulties, such as becoming angry and aggressive

* experience a developmental delay (physically, emotionally and mentally)

* experience school-related problems (eg loss of concentration, even refusing to go to school altogether)

* develop low self-esteem and lack confidence

* suffer depression or inflict self-harm, sometimes leading to suicide attempts

* become withdrawn or introverted

* suffer temporary, or even permanent, injury.

## 2.5 Incidence of Abuse

How many children are abused?

The NSPCC website provides statistical information about child abuse and advice about child protection. In 2015 there were 57,367 children in the UK on child protection registers or the subject of child protection plans on 31 March 2015 (or 31 July 2015 in Scotland):

- England: **49,690**
- Northern Ireland: **1969**
- Scotland: **2772**
- Wales: **2936**

### Incidence of Child Abuse Among Under 18s[23]

- Nearly a quarter of young adults[24] (24.1%) had experienced sexual abuse (including physical and non-physical) by an adult or a peer during childhood.
- One in nine young adults (11.5%) had experienced severe physical violence during childhood at the hands of an adult.

- One in six young adults (16%) had been neglected at some point during childhood and nearly one in 10 (9%) had experienced severe neglect.
- One in 14 young adults (6.9%) experienced emotional abuse during childhood.
- Nearly one in four young adults (23.7%) were exposed to domestic violence between adults in their homes during childhood.

In England, a child protection register is no longer held, but information is collected on children who are the subject of a child protection plan. Child protection plans contain confidential details of children who are at continuing risk of physical, emotional or sexual abuse or neglect. They are managed locally by children's services departments, which coordinate the plan, involving other agencies and individuals in the child's life.

These figures clearly demonstrate a high level of officially recorded abuse across the UK. Some changes in the rates recorded within individual categories reflect alterations in the way in which data is collated and recorded.

Research in 2011[25] explored the incidence of abuse and harm within sport. Table 2 summarises the findings of this report.

[23] Radford, L., Corral, S., Bradley, C., Fisher, H., Bassett, C., Howat, N. and Collishaw, S. (2011) 'Child abuse and neglect in the UK today'. London: NSPCC.

[24] 'Young adults' refers to respondents aged 18–24 at the time of the study talking about their experiences in childhood.

[25] Alexander, K., Stafford, A. and Lewis, R. (2011) *The Experiences of Children Participating in Organised Sport in the UK.* Edinburgh: The University of Edinburgh/NSPCC Centre for UK-wide Learning in Child Protection. ISBN: 978-1-908055-04-0.

**Table 2: Experience of various types of harm in main or second sport, by gender**

|  | All | | Male | | Female | |
|---|---|---|---|---|---|---|
|  | % | Number | % | Number | % | Number |
| Emotional harm | 75% | 4554 | 77% | 1260 | 74% | 3294 |
| Sexual harassment | 29% | 1784 | 17% | 284 | 34% | 1500 |
| Physical harm | 24% | 1433 | 26% | 425 | 23% | 1008 |
| Self-harm | 10% | 605 | 9% | 152 | 10% | 453 |
| Sexual harm | 3% | 171 | 5% | 77 | 2% | 94 |

In summary:

- 75% of respondents reported emotional harm

- 29% reported sexual harassment

- 24% reported physical harm

- 10% reported self-harm

- 3% reported sexual harm.

Child abuse can happen to children of all ages, regardless of their gender, race, culture or background.

**Remember!**

Some children are particularly at risk of harm for various reasons:

**Deaf and disabled children** can be made especially vulnerable to abuse in a number of ways:

- the increased likelihood of social isolation
- having fewer outside contacts than non-disabled children, and perhaps having limited access to someone to disclose to
- a dependency on others for practical assistance in daily living, including intimate care
- an impaired capacity to resist, avoid or understand abuse
- their speech and language communication needs may make it difficult to tell others what is happening
- their particular vulnerability to bullying
- being viewed as an easy target for abusers
- their relative powerlessness (perhaps physically, psychologically and socially) and the opportunities this presents for grooming by potential abusers
- many young people having learnt to be compliant
- a reluctance to challenge carers who may often be viewed as valiantly coping with the burden of a disabled child and therefore not considered as potential risks
- the denial of the possibility of (particularly sexual) abuse of disabled children
- disabled children being less likely to be heard or listened to.

**Children from minority ethnic groups** who are being abused, and who may also be experiencing racial discrimination, may find it hard to tell someone because they feel doubly powerless. The identification of concerns about children from minority ethnic groups may be confused by stereotypes and assumptions that prevent adults reporting concerns.

**Young talented and elite athletes** are particularly vulnerable to abuse. Research[26] has found that, within elite sport, the intensity of the coach-athlete relationship can facilitate power and obedience, and potentially the rationalisation of abuse, which can be more prevalent at the elite level. Talented and elite young athletes often rely heavily on their coaches for many aspects of their life, not just sporting ones. Coaches' decisions are frequently key to progressing in a sport career and reaching goals. This involvement, in combination with the great dependence that often develops, can lead to a blurry or unhealthy coach–athlete relationship. If, in addition, the coach is well respected and has a good reputation based on prior sport successes, this can silence an athlete, perhaps generating denial, preventing them from speaking out, even blaming other athletes who have spoken out about the coach. Talented athletes are more likely to experience[26a]:

- win-at-all-costs approach – elite sport culture is often characterised by this approach. It has been suggested that total adherence to this approach can lead to normalisation of unacceptable risks, uncritical acceptance of negative behaviour and a willingness to do 'whatever it takes'
- status confusion – alongside competing at a high level come demands that are usually associated with adult life; frequent travel trips and being abroad for long periods of time, resulting in separation from family and friendship support, often from a young age; money issues like sponsorship deals or contracts; coping with negative media coverage; balancing intense sport activity with school and other aspects of their life. Athletes can become absorbed by the adult ethos prevailing in many elite sports, and are often treated accordingly by their peers, coaches, parents and members of the entourage
- self-image – on a personal level, and fed by total dedication to their sport, elite young athletes may link their self-image very closely with performance excellence. Given the pressure and expectations to achieve, a failure to reach sport goals can cause their self-esteem to crumble. In highly competitive environments this can make the young athlete vulnerable to all kinds of harmful behaviours from themselves, their coach, parents or members of the entourage.

---

[26] Rhind, D. (2010) 'Towards an understanding of the maintenance of unhealthy coach-athlete relationships' in Brackenridge, C.H. and Rhind, D. (eds) *Elite Child Athlete Welfare*. London: Brunel University Press. ISBN: 978-1-902316-83-3. pp. 101–107.

[26a] Publication of the European Safeguarding Youth Sport (SYS) project, International Centre Ethics in Sport

## 2.6 Identifying Indicators of Abuse

Recognising abuse is not easy, even for individuals who are experienced in working in this field. Often, personal feelings of shock or anger can interfere with the recognition that abuse is, or may be, taking place, and it is easy to deny that it is happening. This section is not designed to make you an expert, but to make you more alert to the signs of possible abuse or poor practice. By the end, you should be able to identify the possible indicators of abuse.

> **Remember!**
>
> It is not your responsibility to decide whether abuse has taken place – it is your responsibility to report your concerns.

### ACTIVITY 18

Jot down any signs that would make you concerned that a child is being abused. An example has been given to start you off.

*Example*

*Change in the child's behaviour from happy child to withdrawn and upset.*

See page 91 for activity feedback.

### Neglect

Because neglect involves adults consistently or regularly failing to meet a child's basic physical and/or psychological needs, it is likely to result in serious impairment of the child's health or development. It can go unnoticed for a long time, yet have lasting and very damaging effects on children. Children who do not receive adequate food or physical care will often develop and mature more slowly, while those who are left alone, unsupervised or unoccupied will often find it difficult to make friends or socialise adequately. It is important to be able to recognise both physical and emotional signs.

**Remember!**

**Physical signs** of neglect include:

- constant hunger, sometimes begging or stealing food from other children
- an unkempt state (frequently dirty or smelly)
- loss of weight or being constantly underweight
- inappropriate dress.

**Behavioural signs** of neglect include:

- being tired all the time
- frequently being late for school or not going to school at all
- failing to attend hospital or medical appointments
- having few friends
- being left alone or unsupervised on a regular basis.

## ACTIVITY 19

Read Sarah's story, then answer the questions provided.

Sarah is a 15-year-old wheelchair fencer. She lives with her father following her parents' divorce two years ago. Sarah has been fencing for three years and has been chosen to take part in an international event in a few months' time.

Sarah misses the first couple of training sessions then turns up but is very unresponsive in the third meeting. Sarah is usually quite shy but generally becomes more animated when discussing fencing. When this is raised with Sarah, she says her father is not able to bring her to meetings, and they had a row about this before he brought her to this meeting.

No one arrives to collect Sarah from this third training session so, with the agreement of the other coaches, you offer to give her a lift home. When you arrive, it is 8pm. Her father takes some time to answer the door, and appears unsteady on his feet and not to fully understand who you are when he does arrive. Sarah invites you in, and the house smells strongly of alcohol and cigarettes. Sarah says she cannot offer you a drink as they are out of milk and mentions that she is hungry and has not eaten since lunchtime. Sarah's father withdraws into another room and does not offer to help.

1   What are the risks for Sarah in this situation?

2   What do you think you might do in this situation?

See page 91 for activity feedback.

## Physical Abuse

Most children will collect cuts and bruises in their daily life, and certainly through their involvement in sport.

**ACTIVITY 20**

1   Jot down the typical soft tissue injuries likely to be sustained in your sport. (Soft tissue refers to tissues that connect, support or surround other structures and organs of the body that are not bone.)

2   Note any areas where you might expect abrasions and bruising from participation in your sport.

**See page 92 for activity feedback.**

## ACTIVITY 21

Read Ben's story, then answer the questions below.

Ben is a 12-year-old boxer who is attending additional boxing sessions over the school holidays. Ben is one of four children living with his parents, Chris and Jane, who both have busy jobs in finance. Ben is usually accompanied to boxing sessions by his older brother, Jim, aged 15.

Yesterday, Ben had a bruise on his cheek, which he kept rubbing. When asked how this had happened, he said he and Jim had been practising their boxing at home and Jim had punched him. You responded by talking to both boys about appropriate boxing practice and explaining the dangers of punching certain areas. Jim became angry, saying it was OK for his father to practise boxing on him, but not for him to practise on Ben.

1   Do you think there are any concerns about these boys? If so, why?

2   What would you do?

See page 92 for activity feedback.

### Physical abuse in sport

In sports where advantages are gained by delaying the onset of puberty (eg the potential strength/weight advantages of prepubescent female gymnasts), drugs and diet may be used to delay physical and sexual development. This may result in serious medical disorders, such as anorexia or osteoporosis.

In other sports where strength, power or speed are key attributes, there is potential for abuse from the use of performance-enhancing drugs.

In sports where participants qualify to compete in weight-based categories (eg boxing, judo), there can be risks of harm to young competitors who are required to sweat off weight in a very short time shortly before competing. There may be serious medical consequences associated with severe dehydration, together with obvious risks in competing in a weakened condition.

In any sport, there is also the potential for physical abuse from overuse injuries. Children should avoid training or competing when suffering from injury, or before injury or illness rehabilitation has been fully completed.

Jot down any other form of potential physical abuse that occurs or may occur in your sport:

## Sexual Abuse

Concerns about sexual abuse are most likely to be detected through changes in a child's behaviour. Concerns may be reported to you by a third party (eg a friend of the child, or another adult who has heard or noticed something that gives rise for concern). Children may tell you either directly or indirectly that they are being sexually abused. Direct disclosures from children are comparatively rare. This will have taken enormous courage on their part because it is likely that they will feel ashamed, afraid, confused and may have been threatened by the abuser. They may be aware, and very frightened, of the potential consequences of disclosing the abuse (eg being told by the abuser that they will be taken to prison or that the child will be taken into 'care'). In all cases, children will tell you because they want the abuse to stop. Therefore, it is very important that you listen to them and take them seriously.

**Remember!**

There may be **physical signs** of sexual abuse, such as:

- pain or itching in the genital area
- bruising or bleeding near the genital area
- having a sexually transmitted disease
- vaginal discharge or infection
- stomach pains
- discomfort when walking or sitting down
- pregnancy.

**If you suspect or become aware of such signs, it is inappropriate for you to check them out yourself. In these circumstances, always refer the child to a medical expert and discuss your concerns with your club welfare or safeguarding officer.**

The sort of **behavioural signs** you may notice include:

- sudden or unexplained changes in behaviour (eg becoming aggressive or withdrawn)
- apparent fear of someone
- running away from home
- having nightmares
- having sexual knowledge that is beyond the child's age or developmental level
- making sexual drawings or using sexual language
- wetting the bed
- having eating problems, such as overeating or anorexia
- self-harming or mutilating, sometimes leading to suicide attempts
- saying they have secrets they cannot tell anyone about
- abusing substances or drugs
- suddenly having unexplained sources of money
- taking over a parental role at home and seeming beyond their age level
- not being allowed to have friends (particularly in adolescence)
- acting in a sexually explicit way towards adults or other young people
- a child telling someone about the abuse.

As with all possible signs of abuse, it is important that these are seen as part of a pattern as, separately, they may have alternative explanations.

## ACTIVITY 23

Read the following story, then answer the questions below.

Linda is a 13-year-old girl with moderate learning difficulties. She receives additional support at school and has recently become involved in her local rounders group, which she enjoys. At rounders, she starts to talk to the coach about life at home. She talks enthusiastically about spending time with her mother but says she does not like Peter, her mother's boyfriend. She appears afraid to say more. As she becomes more confident, she starts to hug her coach regularly and, on one occasion, tries to kiss her on the mouth. When the coach says this isn't appropriate, Linda is surprised and says that was how Peter kissed her. She becomes upset and angry when challenged.

1 Do you have any concerns about Linda? If so, what are they?

2 What do you think you might do at this stage?

See page 93 for activity feedback.

## Emotional Abuse

Emotional abuse is perhaps the most difficult of all forms of abuse to measure. Often, children who appear well cared for may be emotionally abused by being taunted, put down or belittled, or because they receive little or no love, affection or attention from their parents. Coaches and others involved in performance sport should also consider the potential emotional abuse from excessive pressure during training regimes or in relation to competition.

**Remember!**

**Physical signs** of emotional abuse may include:

- a failure to thrive or grow, particularly if the child puts on weight in other circumstances (eg when in hospital or away from their home environment)
- sudden speech disorders
- developmental delay, either in terms of physical or emotional progress.

**Behavioural signs** may include:

- being unable to play, unwilling to take part
- excessive fear of making mistakes
- sudden speech disorders
- self-harm or mutilation
- fear of parents being contacted.

## ACTIVITY 24

Read the following story, then answer the questions below.

Huan is an 11-year-old girl who has a talent for gymnastics. She is Chinese and came to live in England with her parents two years ago. She attends a local gymnastics club and receives support and encouragement from her parents.

One of your fellow coaches at the gymnastics club, George, usually coaches Huan. He is particularly impressed with her abilities and starts to encourage her to attend the club for additional sessions. On one occasion, you arrive early, and George is giving Huan individual tuition. You overhear him berating her for her poor understanding of some of the English terms he is using. He tells Huan she is not trying and is a waste of space. Huan becomes increasingly lacklustre throughout the session and, as a consequence, performs less well. When George sees you, he says, in front of Huan, that she is useless and not worth all the extra attention he is giving her. Huan is nearly in tears at this point but tries to hide this when the other children arrive.

1    What feelings does this raise for you?

2    Do you have concerns about the way George is behaving? Can you identify any examples of poor practice?

3    What action will you take?

See page 93 for activity feedback.

## Bullying

The damage inflicted by bullying is frequently underestimated. It can cause considerable distress to children, to the extent that it affects their health and development or, in extreme cases, causes them significant harm (including self-harm or attempted suicide).

**Remember!**

**Physical signs** of bullying may include:

- stomach aches or headaches
- scratches or bruising
- damaged clothes
- bingeing (eg on food, cigarettes or alcohol)
- a shortage of money
- fatigue (from a lack of sleep)
- frequent loss of possessions.

**Behavioural signs** may include:

- fear and/or avoidance of a particular individual or group
- reduced concentration
- becoming withdrawn or depressed
- being clingy
- emotional fluctuations or mood swings (eg tearful)
- a reluctance to go to school/training
- a drop in performance in sport or at school
- self-harm or attempted suicide.

## 2.7 Summary

In this section, you have had the chance to consider your own feelings about child protection issues and been encouraged to consider specific situations. You have also been asked to consider the different categories of abuse and should now be able to relate them to your own sport.

The signs outlined in Section 2.6 are very important but, even if children display some or all of these signs, it does not necessarily mean they are being abused.

Where you have concerns about a child or an adult's behaviour, it is important to remember that your observations could be the missing piece in a larger jigsaw of concerns that is already being pieced together by child protection professionals, such as social workers and the police. This is why it is vital that you are aware of all the signs, both in terms of what you see (ie physical signs) and in what you observe (ie behavioural signs).

Child abuse, particularly sexual abuse, can arouse strong emotions in those facing such a situation. It is important to acknowledge and understand these emotions and not allow them to interfere with your judgement about what action to take.

In the last few activities in this section, you started to think about what you might do in certain situations. Section 3 takes this a little further and considers what steps to take if you think a child is being abused.

**Remember!**

It is not your responsibility to decide if abuse is happening. However, it is your responsibility to act by reporting your concerns if you suspect abuse.

# 3.0 Introduction

You should always take immediate action by reporting your concerns if a child says or indicates that they are being abused, or if you have reason to suspect that this is the case.

In this section, you will be encouraged to consider how you should respond to a child about whom you have concerns, either as a result of a disclosure from the child, your own observations or the concerns of others. You will also see that, by developing procedures to both prevent and deal with such situations, it is possible to provide both a fun and safe sporting environment for children.

By the end of this section, you should be able to:

* describe how you would respond to a child who discloses abuse

* recognise the importance of your own observations in the detection of possible abuse

* identify the person(s) to whom you should report or share your concern

* deal with difficult situations involving allegations against parents or other staff/volunteers

* deal with incidents of bullying

* describe the responsibilities of various agencies/organisations, including your club, governing bodies of sport, local authorities, children's services and the police

* prepare yourself for the possibility of having to deal with suspected abuse in the future.

# 3.1 Responding to Observations or Concerns

## Children

Due to the nature of coaching, you have a unique opportunity to observe children both physically and emotionally. For example, coaches may be ideally placed to recognise concerns about changes in a young person's general demeanour, or their physical and psychological development and welfare. However, it is not your role to investigate or assess child protection concerns, but to report them using the appropriate procedures. (Always remember to obtain parents' consent to collect relevant medical and other information when a child joins your club.)

## Colleagues

Remember, you not only have to consider the consequences of your own actions, but also those of others within your club. For example, from time to time, you may be required to observe other coaches' sessions and may have concerns or spot risks that, for whatever reason, have been missed by the coach leading the session. In these circumstances, you may need to intervene, either by stopping the session or simply discussing your concerns with the coach in question. This should be viewed as good practice, rather than interfering, as a failure to take action could result in a child being injured or a case of negligence being made against the coach and/or club. The incident should be recorded in writing and made available to other coaches so they can avoid making the same mistake themselves.

Whereas some incidents are clearly a cause for concern and may prompt action (such as a risk assessment, change to coaching style or review of goals), be aware that some incidents are not so obvious and only surface once the damage has occurred.

## Dealing with Bullying

All incidents or suspicions of bullying must be taken very seriously. Many clubs now have guidelines and procedures to place clear expectations and procedures around dealing with bullying so it is worth checking with your club for the appropriate process. The guidelines in the box below will also help your club deal with the issue appropriately:

### How to deal with bullying

- Develop guidelines on dealing with bullying and ensure these are part of an active policy.

- Involve children in the development and review of these guidelines and procedures.

- Consider the impact of social networking within guidelines as this is often a neglected area where bullying frequently takes place.

- Promote the guidelines in your club's code of practice.

- Ensure that the concepts of equity, value and inclusion are covered in staff training.

- Take all signs of bullying seriously.

- Involve parents.

- Do not ignore the victim or bully – encourage them to discuss their thoughts both with you and, if appropriate, others within the group.

- Encourage the children involved to change their behaviour in order to improve the situation.

- If a disclosure is made to you, remember to listen to and reassure the victim, record your conversation and report to the appropriate person.

- Invite professional organisations to explain specific issues to children and offer further help – this could be a session for both coaches and children.

- Share concerns – the victim may not be safe.

- Follow up what you do – remember that sport should be safe and fun for both the victim and bully.

- If the bullying incident was severe in nature (eg a serious assault), or bullying behaviour persists despite attempts to deal with it, this should be reported and dealt with in line with the club's child protection policy and procedures (including consideration of the need to refer the matter to statutory services).

## 3.2 Responding to Disclosures and Reports of Abuse

### Sources of Concern

Concerns may arise in a number of ways:

- a direct disclosure of abuse to you

- a conversation with an adult (eg a parent, spectator or colleague) or another child

- direct observation of a worrying incident

- observation of signs or behaviour that suggest possible abuse

- receipt of an anonymous allegation (eg by phone, text, email or letter).

### Disclosure by a Child

A disclosure is when a child or another person tells you that they believe they have been the victim of abuse or someone else has.

Children who are being abused rarely tell anyone (disclose) directly, and then will usually only tell people they trust and with whom they feel safe. Coaches very often share a close relationship with their participants and may, therefore, be the sort of person in whom a child might place their trust.

Children want the abuse to stop. By listening and taking what a child is telling you seriously, you will already be helping to protect them.

It is useful to think in advance about how you might respond to this situation in such a way as to support the child while complying with the relevant code of practice. The following guidelines are included in most governing bodies of sport child protection policies and procedures, and it is strongly recommended that they are incorporated into those of your own club.

### Timing and location

Understandably, a child who has been abused may want to see you alone, away from others. This may be before or after a session, and it is important to consider this child's needs alongside the needs of other children in the activity. Therefore, you may also need to attend to other children, check equipment or set up an activity – you cannot simply leave a session unattended. You may want to try to arrange to speak to the child at an appropriate time or arrange for assistance for your session.

Location is very important. Although it is important to respect the child's need for privacy, you also need to protect yourself against misinterpretation or potential allegations. Do not listen to the child's disclosure in a completely private place – try to ensure other members of staff are present or at least nearby.

## Responding to the child

It will have taken a great deal of courage for a child to tell you about abusive behaviour, and it is crucial that you take this into consideration when responding to the child's disclosure. Following the guidance in the box below will help you to act in an appropriate and responsible manner.

**Guidance on responding to a child**

- Do not panic – react calmly so as not to frighten the child.

- Acknowledge that what the child is doing is difficult, but that they are right to confide in you.

- Reassure the child that they are not to blame.

- Make sure that, from the outset, you can understand what the child is saying.

- Be honest straight away and tell the child you cannot make promises that you will not be able to keep.

- Do not promise that you will keep the conversation a secret. Explain that, in order to help them, you will need to involve other people and that you will need to write things down.

- Listen carefully to the child; take them seriously.

- Do not allow your shock or distaste to show.

- Keep any questions to the minimum required for you to clarify any facts or words that you do not understand – do not speculate or make assumptions.

- Do not probe for more information than is offered as this may affect any future investigation by statutory agencies.

- Encourage the child to use their own words.

- Do not make negative comments about the alleged abuser.

- At the end of the conversation, ensure that the child is either being collected or is capable of going home on their own.

- Do not approach the alleged abuser.

## Responding to reports and observations that cause concern

It is important to take all reports of concerns and observations that lead to concerns seriously. Make a note of any concerns, seek support and use your organisational procedures to report these.

All concerns should be recorded using an incident report form. You should use your governing body/club's standard incident report form or the sample form opposite as a template.

Once you have completed the written record:

- sign and date it

- provide your club welfare officer and others with copies, as required by your club's safeguarding/child protection procedures

- store the information in accordance with your club or governing body of sport procedures (as a minimum, somewhere safe and secure).

## Safeguarding incident report form

Child's name: ................................................................ Date of birth: ...............................................

Address: ...............................................................................................................................................

...................................................................................... Postcode: ........................................................

Disability/relevant medical condition: ...................................... Ethnicity: ........................................

Home/parent's name and telephone number: .......................................................................................

Sports club/school child attends: ............................................................................................................

Date of incident/report/disclosure: .......................................................................................................

Time: ......................................................... Venue: .........................................................................

If concerns were passed on by a third party, supply their details (name, contact number etc), and record what was said:

......................................................................................................................................................

*(Continue overleaf if necessary.)*

If the child/young person made a direct disclosure, describe the circumstances and record what the child said

(using their words): ...............................................................................................................................

......................................................................................................................................................

*(Continue overleaf if necessary.)*

If concerns arise from your observations/actions, give details: .............................................................

......................................................................................................................................................

Name, role, relationship to the child, and contact details (if known) of any alleged abuser(s):

......................................................................................................................................................

Name, role and contact details of any potential witnesses to the alleged incident:

......................................................................................................................................................

Any actions that you have taken (include name, role, agency and contact number for person[s] with whom this

information has been shared, including parents, and any agreed actions): .............................................

......................................................................................................................................................

Your name: ........................................................................ Role: ..................................................

Contact number: ...................................................................................................................................

Signature: ..............................................................................................................................................

Pass this form on to: ............................................................................... in line with your club's procedures.

Please ensure confidentiality and share your concerns on a strict need-to-know basis, and only in order to protect this child or other children.

You may wish to seek reassurance by discussing your concerns with someone outside the club.

The NSPCC provides a free, 24-hour service on **0808-800 5000**.

## Sharing Your Concerns

As a result of a disclosure or an observation, you may be worried about what a child has said or simply have a feeling that something is not quite right. Taking action in cases of child abuse is never easy, and you will inevitably experience a mixture of emotions. You may feel that you have been partly responsible; you may be worried about the consequences of the action you take for the child's family or others. These feelings are completely natural, particularly because of the nature of the media's coverage of child abuse.

What is important is the child's long-term future – imagine what could happen if you do not take action. Sadly, in some extreme cases, a failure to act has led to a child's death, as many child abuse enquiries have shown. At the very least, a failure to act may well result in the continuing abuse of one or more children. Your information could be vital in preventing further abuse, and you have a responsibility to share and/or report your concerns, however small they may be. Many adult survivors of childhood abuse have said that telling someone who helped stop the abuse was a vital step in the healing process. Even though parents may not be happy about initial referrals being made to statutory authorities, they appreciate honesty and transparency and are often glad to have received help and support at a time of crisis.

### Sharing with a designated person, welfare/safeguarding officer or senior colleague

In some sport situations, it may be quite easy to determine who you should contact if you are concerned about a child being abused. This will be detailed in the child protection or safeguarding policy for the club if this is available.

- If you work for a local authority, in a sport or leisure centre, or at a school, there should be staff with designated child protection responsibilities.

- If not, you will have a senior colleague or line manager (the person to whom you are directly responsible/your employer/the person who appointed you) to contact. Alternatively, contact the NSPCC on 0808-800 5000.

- If your work with children takes place at a sports club, your governing body of sport is likely to have a lead child protection officer, and your club should have a club welfare officer, to whom you can report your concerns.

- Failing this, you should speak to the club secretary or chairperson.

Whether you are a paid employee or volunteer, there should be someone to whom you can turn.

However, in some circumstances, particularly if you work in a voluntary capacity, there may be no obvious person to whom you can report any concerns you may have. For example, you may coach at a club operating after school or for a local team on a Saturday morning. In these cases, it is particularly important to plan what you would do if you suspected abuse before you are actually faced with a real-life situation.

### Remember!

Whoever you talk to, you will need to maintain confidentiality, but do not need to take full responsibility. Your lead child protection officer, club welfare officer or senior colleague will expect to be informed so you can begin to take action that will enable others to protect the child and provide support in what could be a difficult situation.

### Sharing with parents

You should always be committed to working in partnership with parents when there are concerns about their children. In most situations, it is therefore important to talk to parents to help clarify any initial concerns. In doing so, you may discover reasons that explain behavioural changes or find out that the family needs further support. Parents will usually inform someone at your club if their child is upset or unwell, but occasionally, this information may not reach you. In cases like this, simply talking to parents can help to resolve any initial concerns.

In some circumstances it is not advisable to share concerns with parents. For example there may be indications or suspicions that the parents may be responsible for or have otherwise allowed the suspected abuse; or there may be fears that a parent's response may further harm the child or impact on a potential statutory agency investigation. If so, seek advice from the welfare officer, a senior colleague or statutory services.

If the concerns are about someone who also plays a role within sport, then the club welfare officer or a senior colleague should inform the relevant sporting organisation's lead child protection/safeguarding officer, in line with agreed procedures.

## Sharing with professionals

In some situations, particularly if it would be inappropriate to discuss your concerns with the child's parents, it may be necessary to inform children's services and/or the police. If available, your organisational lead child protection/safeguarding officer, club welfare officer or senior colleague/line manager should take responsibility for this. However, you need to be aware of what to do in case they are unavailable or inappropriate (eg the concerns relate to this person), or there is no one obvious to whom you can report your concerns. The process is as follows:

1  Inform the duty officer at children's services or the police and explain that your referral involves child protection. (If your referral refers to concerns about someone in a position of responsibility, ask to speak to the local authority designated officer[27] who coordinates these referrals.) Give your name, role, address and telephone number (this is helpful rather than required). Give clear, accurate details of the child (ie name, address and date of birth), what you have observed (include date and time, details of the child's behaviour and emotional state), what the child has said, and what action you have taken. This is the type of information you should have recorded on the incident report form (from your club/governing body of sport or the sample form on page 63).

2  Children's services/the police will advise you on what to do next, including whether, how and when to involve parents, and will also take responsibility for ensuring appropriate enquiries and investigations are undertaken.

3  If a child needs urgent medical attention as a result of suspected abuse, then you must seek this as a matter of urgency. Inform medical staff of your suspicions of possible abuse and contact children's services as soon as possible to obtain advice about involving parents.

4  Record carefully what you have heard, seen and done, including conversations you have had with other professionals, using the appropriate incident report form (see point 1). Send or hand the completed report form to the appropriate safeguarding/welfare lead in line with your club's safeguarding procedures.

### Remember!

- However small your concern, share it with your club welfare officer, organisational lead child protection officer or senior colleague/line manager, who will take responsibility for deciding the next steps and whether to inform statutory services or other organisations. If no one is available (or your concern is about this person), then you must ring the statutory services yourself, giving accurate details of your concerns.

- Children's services have a responsibility to respond to all concerns about possible child abuse; they will decide with the police whether an investigation is needed.

- It is important to be open and honest with parents, but in some circumstances, this may put the child in more danger. If in doubt, discuss your concerns first with appropriate and qualified personnel.

[27] England only.

The diagram below offers some guidelines on how to respond to concerns about a child being harmed outside the sport environment.

Concerns emerge about possible abuse of a child outside the sport through a disclosure by the child, reports from others or observations. If necessary, ensure the immediate safety of the child (and other children).
Report concerns to the relevant club welfare officer, organisational lead safeguarding officer or line manager/senior colleague who will decide what action to take next. It is important not to delay reporting your concerns to statutory services or police if the relevant person within your organisation is not available.
Record concerns using an incident form.
The welfare/safeguarding officer reports concerns to statutory services and liaises with parents.


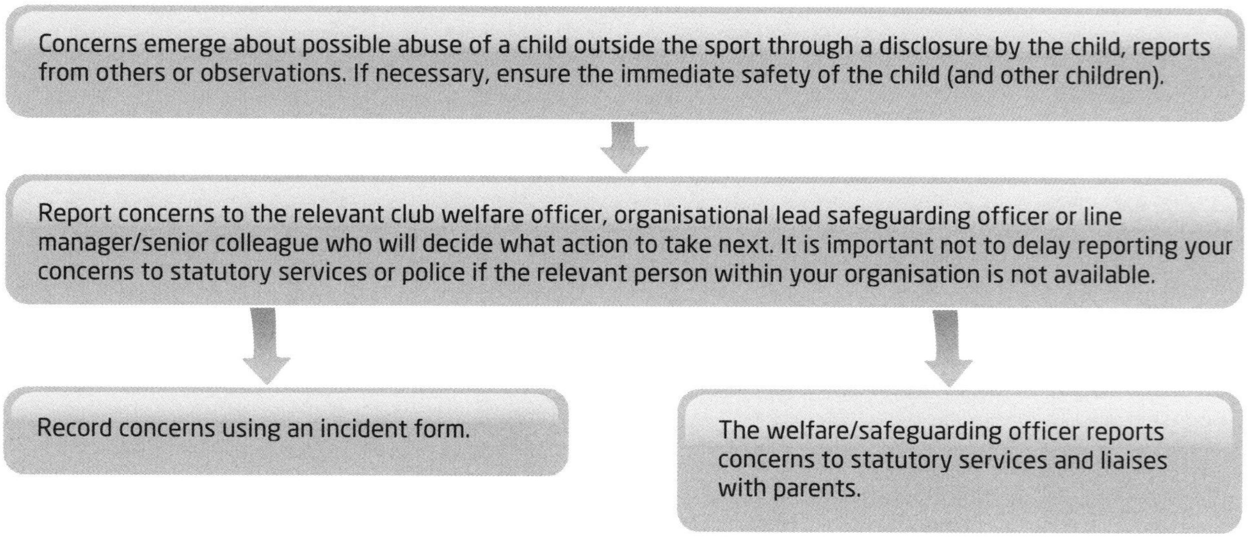

**Figure 3: Responding to concerns outside the sport environment**

The diagram below depicts the distinction between the roles and responsibilities of sports organisations and those of the statutory agencies.

Sports Organisations
Governing bodies of sport, CSPs, clubs etc
Staff/volunteer awareness/ recognition
Reporting arrangements
Complaints/disciplinary processes
Sports organisation's child protection policies and procedures
Referral process to local authority children's social care or police
Information sharing
LADO involvement
Statutory Agencies
Local authority children's social care, police, local authority designated officer (LADO)
Strategy meeting/ investigation
Assessment/ intervention
Child protection conference/plan
Criminal/care proceedings
LSCB child protection policies and procedures


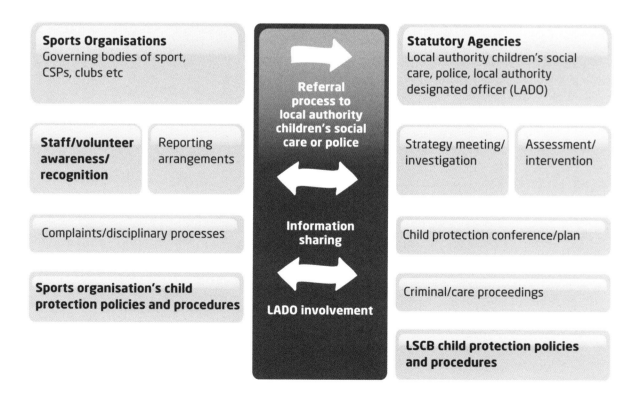

**Figure 4: The role of sports organisations and statutory agencies (© CPSU)**

The diagram below offers some general guidelines on how to respond to any concerns you may have about staff or volunteers in your club. However, these guidelines are by no means definitive – you should also refer to your club or organisation's policy.

If you have concerns about the behaviour of a member of staff or volunteer towards a child/young person, if necessary, ensure the immediate safety of the child (and other children).

Report concerns to the relevant club welfare officer, organisational lead safeguarding officer or line manager/senior colleague (it is important not to delay reporting your concerns to statutory services or police if the relevant person within your organisation is not available) who will decide if the concern constitutes:

**poor practice** and/or breach of organisation's code of practice/ethics.

**possible child abuse.**

Relevant organisational complaints/ disciplinary procedures initiated. Consider consulting with LADO.

Relevant organisational complaints/disciplinary procedures initiated - decision regarding temporary suspension, pending outcome of any statutory investigations and organisation's subsequent disciplinary investigation.

Concerns referred to children's services who involve the police; if concerns relate to someone in a position of responsibility, referral to the LADO (England).

Organisational complaints/ disciplinary investigation undertaken.

Organisational complaints/ disciplinary investigation undertaken, informed by outcome of statutory investigation.

Possible outcomes of process/hearing:
- no case to answer
- warrants advice/warning as to future conduct/sanctions
- further training/support needed
- dismissal and referral to the DBS.

Possible outcomes of process/hearing:
- no case to answer
- warrants advice/warning as to future conduct/sanctions
- further training/support needed
- dismissal and referral to DBS for consideration for barring.

Possible outcomes:
- threshold for statutory investigation not met so referred back to organisation for disciplinary proceedings
- children's services/ police enquiries and investigation
- no case to answer
- criminal proceedings
- possible civil proceedings.

**Appeals** procedure should be available to anyone under investigation as part of natural justice.

**Figure 5: Outline process for responding to concerns about staff/volunteers**

If you do not know who to turn to for advice or are worried about sharing your concerns with someone inside your club, contact children's services directly (or the NSPCC helpline on 0808-800 5000).

**Referrals to statutory agencies**

There may be three types of investigation:

- criminal (police)

- child protection (children's services/police)

- disciplinary (employing/deploying organisation).

Civil proceedings may also be initiated by the alleged victim, their family or the person accused.

The club's designated welfare officer (if available) should make their governing body of sport equivalent aware of the allegation and seek advice as appropriate (eg how to deal with the media). However, if the club's child protection officer is the subject of the allegation, a senior person from the club should report directly to the governing body of sport's lead child protection officer.

The governing body of sport and/or club should make an immediate decision about whether an individual accused of abuse should be temporarily suspended from coaching pending further statutory enquiries.

Irrespective of the findings of children's services or police enquiries, the club must assess all available information in each case, under the appropriate misconduct/disciplinary procedure, to decide whether the accused should be reinstated and, if so, how this can be handled sensitively with other staff or volunteers. The welfare of children should always be the primary consideration, even when there is insufficient evidence either to take the matter to court or secure a conviction. It is important to note that the burden of proof required to secure a conviction is 'beyond reasonable doubt'. This is a higher threshold than that required in child protection/welfare proceedings (including sport organisations' disciplinary and misconduct procedures), where a judgement is made 'on the balance of probability' about whether allegations are true and an individual is a potential risk to children.

## 3.3 Responsibilities of Agencies/Organisations

**Remember!**

If you suspect that a child may be being abused, it is not your responsibility to take control of the situation, nor to investigate/decide whether or not child abuse has actually taken place. However, you do have a responsibility to report your concerns and ensure the safety of the children under your supervision.

### Your Club

- Your club should have a child protection or safeguarding policy and procedures document that explains the process to follow. This will make clear who to contact and what action to take in the event of concerns about a child. This information should be clearly communicated to all club members.

- Your club should identify a designated person to lead on safeguarding and manage child protection issues. The designated person will require support from your club and/or the wider organisation and receive appropriate training. This support should be provided as part of the child protection policy and implementation procedures adopted by your club.

### Governing Bodies of Sport

- Governing bodies of sport should have in place and publish safeguarding/child protection policies, procedures and codes of practice and ethics.

- A lead designated officer should be appointed to develop safeguarding practice and knowledge within the organisation.

- Established systems should be in place to facilitate the safe recruitment of staff and volunteers, including criminal records checks, where relevant.

- Case management systems should be established to coordinate and manage reported concerns consistently.

- Designated safeguarding officers should be provided with support and training to enable them to respond appropriately to concerns and refer them to statutory authorities.

- Coaches should be provided with support and advice in areas such as recruitment, insurance, first aid and sport-specific issues with regard to good safeguarding practice.

## Local Authorities

- Local authorities have specific legal duties in respect of the Children Acts 1989 and 2004, the Children (Scotland) Act 1995, the Protection of Children Act 1999, the Safeguarding Vulnerable Groups Act 2006 and the Protection of Freedoms Act 2012.

- They work to safeguard the welfare of children in partnership with other public agencies, the voluntary sector, service users, parents and professional carers. Local authorities have the lead responsibility to provide effective services for children in need. In England and Wales, LSCBs provide multi-agency forums to manage and oversee safeguarding across the local authority. In England, local authority designated officers (often known as LADOs) coordinate referrals of concerns about people in positions of trust, including sports coaches.

- Local authorities are often involved in play or activity scheme provision. You may be coaching or working in a play/activity scheme, either during a school holiday or for a specific programme. Many local authorities will provide the expertise of a community sports coordinator to make sure all those involved in such coaching activities have access to the most appropriate resources, including coach education.

- Detailed safeguarding and child protection policies and procedures should also be produced by all local authorities. They should provide guidance on all aspects of good practice and child protection for coaches, staff and volunteers.

- CSPs operate in each local authority and coordinate/promote safeguarding information, among other functions, for sports organisations in that locality. They also have safeguarding policies and procedures and appoint a lead designated safeguarding officer.

## Children's Services

- Children's services (called social care or social services in some areas) provide a wide range of care and support for children and families. This includes support to children with physical or learning disabilities and mental health problems; young offenders; families, especially where children have special needs; children at risk of harm; children who need to be accommodated or looked after by the local authority through fostering or residential care; and children who are placed for adoption.

- Children's services have a statutory duty to ensure the welfare of children. In England and Wales, this includes working with LSCBs and, in Scotland, with the local child protection committee to comply with procedures for responding to and managing child protection referrals and cases.

- When a child protection referral is made, children's services have a legal responsibility to make enquiries if they have reason to suspect that a child in their area is suffering, or is likely to suffer, significant harm. They will work closely with the police.

- Children's services coordinate an assessment of the:
  - child's needs
  - parents' capacity to keep the child safe
  - parents' capacity to promote the child's welfare
  - wider family circumstances.

- Statutory agencies share information appropriately with one another so children's services share information with the police and significant others (eg health or education authorities). In some cases, this may include information from a sports club or members of its staff.

- Where the child is thought to be in immediate danger, children's services may apply to the courts for emergency powers to ensure a child's safety by placing them under the protection of the local authority. The police also have powers to take children into police protection in an emergency.

- Because of their responsibilities, duties and powers in relation to vulnerable children, children's services act as the principle point of contact for children if there are child welfare concerns. They may also be contacted directly by parents, family members seeking help, concerned friends, neighbours and professionals, or others from statutory and voluntary agencies.

**Police**

The police have two primary duties:

1  To prevent crime and protect the public – within this, they recognise the fundamental importance of inter-agency working in combating child abuse. All forces have child abuse investigation units and, despite variations in their structure, they will normally take primary responsibility for investigating child abuse cases where a crime is alleged.

2  Emergency powers to enter premises and ensure the immediate protection of children believed to be suffering, or at risk of, significant harm – at the conclusion of their investigation, the police will pass their file to the Crown Prosecution Service (CPS) in England or the Procurator Fiscal Service (PFS) in Scotland to determine whether criminal proceedings should be initiated.

**Other Agencies/Organisations**

There are a number of additional agencies/organisations that can provide support in making referrals to statutory services – these include:

• ChildLine[28]

• NSPCC helpline[29].

There may also be local support groups in your area that you could approach for guidance, support or practical help.

# 3.4 Taking Preparatory Action

It is important to be prepared for the possibility of having to deal with suspected abuse in the future so, in the event, you are able to respond calmly and appropriately.

The following action points relate to your club's records and are things you should be able to tackle more or less immediately:

• Children's names:
  – Check that names are complete and spelled correctly.
  – Be aware that parents' surnames may be different from that of their children. Establish who has parental responsibility for the child. (This may be one parent or shared by both parents, or another relative.)

• Phone numbers:
  – Check that numbers are up to date and include area codes.
  – Check that mobile numbers are correct.
  – Ensure that you have emergency contact details.

• Addresses:
  – Check that addresses are complete and up to date.
  – If possible, obtain a map of the local area – it is surprising how many people are unfamiliar with it.

• Procedures:
  – Make sure you are familiar with your club/governing body of sport child protection or safeguarding policy and procedures.

[28] ChildLine is available for all children (Tel: 0800-1111).
[29] The NSPCC offers confidential advice to children, young people and adults with concerns (Tel: 0808-800 5000).

Jot down in the space below any additional action points you think would help you:

The following activity will help you compile a list of people to contact in relation to child protection issues. Take a photocopy of your completed list and keep it somewhere safe for future reference.

## ACTIVITY 26

Find out the names and telephone numbers of the main child protection contacts within your club and/or governing body of sport, social services and police service, and record the details below.

**Child protection contacts**

Name of the person in your normal coaching environment to whom you should report any concerns about child protection issues: .........................................................................................................................................................................

Job title: ...............................................................................................................................................................................................

Address: ...............................................................................................................................................................................................

.....................................................................................................................................................................................................................

.............................................................................................Tel: .........................................................................................................

Welfare/safeguarding officer/child protection (if different from above): .........................................................

.....................................................................................................................................................................................................................

Tel: ...........................................................................................................................................................................................................

Organisational lead child protection/safeguarding officer: ...........................................................................................

Tel: ...........................................................................................................................................................................................................

Children's services contact: .....................................................................................................................................................

Tel: ...........................................................................................................................................................................................................

Police station contact: ................................................................................................................................................................

Tel: ...........................................................................................................................................................................................................

Name of local hospital: ..............................................................................................................................................................

Tel: ...........................................................................................................................................................................................................

See page 94 for activity feedback.

## What Would You Do?

In the following activities, you will be asked to consider a series of case studies and scenarios. In some cases, you will be asked to comment on the actions of the people involved; in others, you will be asked to think about how you would respond if you were involved. Remember that making the correct decision is not always straightforward. Refer to the information in this resource or contact more experienced professionals for advice and guidance.

## ACTIVITY 27

### Case Study 1

The following case study has been written from a parent's point of view. As you read through it, jot down your concerns as a coach in the space provided.

Your children want to attend a sports team practice session in your local park every Saturday morning. You agree that they can go, and provide them with some money, sports kits and drinks. As the park is not far away and is near their school, you agree that they can walk there together, unaccompanied, and feel assured that they will be safe. The practice goes well, the children seem keen, and the session is popular, with lots of other children and parents attending.

After a while, the enthusiastic coaches enter a local tournament. As a result of this, even more children turn up to practices, several teams are formed and a request is made to parents to provide a donation in order to buy equipment. You decide to go and watch a practice session – you have not really thought to do so in the past and wish to see the set-up. However, you do not tell your children that you intend to turn up. On arriving at the park, you are disturbed to see lots of children playing sport, but no sign of your own. You spot an adult, but he is just another parent having a game. You begin to get very concerned. It is time for the practice to end and still there is no sign of your children.

More parents gather and you learn that some of the children, including yours, have been taken to play a match on the other side of town – in cars by other parents. Time passes very slowly. It is cold, and you do not really know what to do; it begins to rain, and there is no shelter. You have just about had enough when out of a car step your children, who happily tell you that they won their match in extra time.

You are introduced to the coaches who turn out to be teenagers – they are in the sixth form at school and just love playing sport. They tell you that the best way to keep in touch with what is going on in the club is through the Facebook group where information, photos and coaches' details are posted and members chat to one another.

### Your concerns:

**Case Study 2**

Now compare Case Study 1 with the following, which has also been written from a parent's perspective. As you read through it, jot down any examples of good practice that you come across in the space provided.

Your children want to take up sport on a Saturday morning. You are pleased because there is a well-established local club nearby. You telephone the organiser, who sends you an information pack about the club, in which you are surprised, but pleased, to find several consent forms, a request for information about your children and a statement that sets out the club objectives and code of practice for the coaches. You are asked to complete the documentation and invited to take your children for a trial visit. The documentation includes information about the club's Facebook group, which is available for older members and parents to find out, but not post, information. The following Saturday, you take the children to the club to meet a coach and receive an induction to the centre. You are all very impressed with what you see and are informed that recent Lottery money has enabled the club to invest in coach training, resources and facilities. The club has been awarded Clubmark status. You are also told that, as members, you will have to be involved with the progress of your children and may be asked to contribute to some activities (eg supervising changing rooms, preparing refreshments, joining the club committee, being available for matches, fund-raising events and socials). As you tour the club, you see that some of the younger coaches are working with more experienced ones and are impressed to learn that the club employs qualified staff and makes use of volunteers. The session ends, and you see that all the children are collected by their parents. They appear pleased with the morning's training and are able to speak freely to staff. Both you and your children confirm that you wish to join the club.

**Examples of good practice:**

See pages 94–95 for activity feedback.

This activity is designed to help you check your understanding of good practice and the need for procedures. As you read through the following scenario, jot down any examples of good practice that you come across in the left-hand column of the table below. Then jot down any additional areas of good practice that you think should be adopted in the right-hand column.

As the manager of a local volunteer-run club, you are responsible for recruiting staff. Your committee has approved a proposal to recruit three extra part-time leisure activity staff. You also decide to take the opportunity to recruit volunteers at the same time. You decide to place an advert in the local paper, in which you outline the aims of the club and specific areas of coaching in which you wish to recruit staff. There is an excellent response to the advert, particularly from students at a local college.

As part of your pre-recruitment checks, you send out application forms accompanied by information outlining the qualities and experience required. You also ask candidates to submit a reference. You decide to formally interview several candidates to clarify their qualifications, training needs, previous experience and expectations. At the interviews, you explain that successful candidates will be required to receive training on working with children.

You appoint three members of part-time staff and several volunteers. You explain that they will all receive an induction to the club and regular feedback on their progress.

| Examples of Good Practice | Additional Recommendations |
|---|---|
|  |  |

See page 95 for activity feedback.

The following extracts are from a local sport and leisure club's records. For each one, decide what you would do if you were involved in the situation.

| Situation | What Would You Do? |
|---|---|
| 1  Staff complained that equipment (including trampolines, football goals and badminton posts) was not put away after being used, but just pushed into the corners of the sports hall. The storeroom in the sports hall was full of benches, chairs and cupboards. | |
| 2  One of the club's coaches raised concerns about the behaviour of a group of children attending his session. In the changing room, he discovered that shampoo had been poured into some of the children's bags, shoes had been placed in the shower, and coats had been hidden in the outside bins. He was alerted to this by a parent who said it was not the first time this had happened and her child was unhappy and wished to leave the club. When questioned, none of the children said anything. | |
| 3  One of the senior coaches reported that he was not happy about a younger coach dating a 17-year-old participant. He knew that the relationship had been going on for some time. | |
| 4  Several children attending a sports session ending at 7.30pm were continually being left waiting by their parents until the TV soap operas finished at 8.30pm. The premises were locked at 8.00pm. | |
| 5  A member of staff asked other coaches whether they had noticed a difference in Sarah recently. At the beginning of the season, her weight had been normal for her age. However, she was now looking thin and tired, and often sat out of training sessions. | |

| Situation | What Would You Do? |
|---|---|
| 6 A fixture was abandoned due to the behaviour of the visiting team's parents on the sideline. | |
| 7 A risk assessment at the sport and leisure club revealed a number of problems with the running track, which would make it challenging for all the young people, but in particular a couple of children with cerebral palsy, to use safely. | |
| 8 A coach noticed that one of the younger children had marks that looked like circular burns on his arms during an activity session in which children got hotter than usual and took their jumpers off. The child quickly covered the marks up and seemed very reluctant to discuss them. | |
| 9 A part-time coach started the season well, but soon slipped into a routine of arriving late and getting the children to set out equipment unsupervised. | |
| 10 Several parents felt uneasy about a stranger hanging around the club with a camera. | |

See page 95 for activity feedback.

## 3.5 Summary

In this section, you have been offered guidance on what to do if you suspect a child is being abused, and on the policies and procedures your club should establish and implement in order to promote good practice and protect children.

**Remember!**

- The welfare of the child must be of paramount importance in all issues relating to child protection.

- If a child needs urgent medical attention as a result of suspected abuse, you must seek this as a matter of urgency, then inform the statutory services. Seek advice from children's services before informing parents if you have concerns.

- Talk to parents to clarify concerns about any injury or change in behaviour (unless there are indications that the parents may be harming the child, or the child might otherwise be placed at increased risk by informing them).

- If you are still concerned, follow your organisational child protection procedures and speak to your child protection/safeguarding or welfare officer, or contact the duty officer at children's services or the police. If another coach or volunteer is involved, ensure your governing body of sport is also informed.

- Give clear, accurate details, including the child's name and address, and reasons for your concern.

- Children's services will advise you about what to do next and take responsibility for ensuring appropriate investigations are undertaken if necessary.

- Record carefully what you have seen, heard and done as soon as possible using your club/organisation's incident report form.

- Remember that confidentiality in matters relating to child protection is vital, and information must only be shared with the child protection/safeguarding/welfare officer or senior colleagues (where essential) and child protection professionals.

Remember not to shoulder the burden of child protection on your own. If you are concerned or unsure, always ring children's services, the police or the NSPCC. Their telephone numbers are in the local phone book. The NSPCC offers a free 24-hour national helpline (Tel: 0808-800 5000). There may be issues that you need to discuss with your governing body of sport, employer or organisation – ensure you make arrangements to meet the appropriate personnel. If you require further information or confidential advice (for professional or personal reasons), Section 4 provides an extensive list of useful contacts and recommended further reading in relation to child protection issues.

## 4.0 Introduction

Part of being a good coach is being open to new ideas and training, and keeping skills and knowledge up to date. A good coach would also have the skills to adapt training to meet the needs of individual children and seek advice, where required, in areas outside their expertise.

If you have not already done so, you are strongly recommended to attend sports coach UK's workshop 'Safeguarding and Protecting Children'[30]. If you have attended this, the refresher workshop 'Safeguarding and Protection Children 2: Reflecting on Practice' can help you apply your knowledge and skills in this area.

This section provides a comprehensive list of publications, workshops and organisations that can provide support and guidance on child protection issues.

## 4.1 Further Reading and Resources

The following include a selection of useful publications and websites that support the information provided in this resource.

Alexander, K., Stafford, A. and Lewis, R. (2011) *The Experiences of Children Participating in Organised Sport in the UK*. Edinburgh: The University of Edinburgh/NSPCC Centre for UK-wide Learning in Child Protection. ISBN: 978-1-908055-04-0. (Available via: www.sportscoachuk.org/children-experiences)

Brackenridge, C.H. and Rhind, D. (eds) *Elite Child Athlete Welfare*. London: Brunel University Press. ISBN: 978-1-902316-83-3.

Cassidy, T., Jones, R. and Potrac, P. (2009) *Understanding Sports Coaching: The Social, Cultural and Pedagogical Foundations of Coaching Practice*. 2nd edition. London: Routledge. ISBN: 978-0-415442-72-5.

CPSU (2016) 'Standards for Safeguarding and Protecting Children in Sport'. Leicester: NSPCC National Training Centre. (Available via: www.sportscoachuk.org/spc-standards)

CPSU (2010) 'Club framework for safeguarding standards in sport'. Belfast: NSPCC Northern Ireland. (Available via: www.sportscoachuk.org/club-framework)

CPSU (2012) *Safeguarding Deaf and Disabled Children in Sport* (DVD and CD-ROM). Leicester: NSPCC. (Available via: www.sportscoachuk.org/safeguarding-deaf-disabled)

DfE (2015) *Working Together to Safeguard Children: A guide to inter-agency working to safeguard and promote the welfare of children*. London: DfE. (Available via: www.sportscoachuk.org/inter-agency)

Department for Education and Skills (DfES) (2015) *What to Do if You're Worried a Child is Being Abused*. London: DfES. ISBN: 978-1-844788-67-5. (Available via: www.sportscoachuk.org/abuse-worry)

Lyle, J. (2002) *Sports Coaching Concepts: A Framework for Coaches' Behaviour*. London: Routledge. ISBN: 978-0-415261-58-6.

Lyle, J. and Cushion, C. (2010) *Sports Coaching: Professionalisation and Practice*. Oxford: Churchill Livingstone. ISBN: 978-0-702030-54-3.

McInulty, K. (2006) 'Creating a Safe Environment for Children in Sport: Scottish Governing Bodies Child Protection Guidelines'. 2nd edition. Glasgow: CHILDREN 1ST.

Oliver, J.L., Lloyd, R.S. and Meyers, R.W. (2011) 'Training elite child athletes: promoting welfare and wellbeing', *Strength and Conditioning Journal*, 33 (4): 73–79.

Prescott, P. and Hartill, M. (2007) 'Safeguarding children in sport: A view from rugby league – the policy process, participative cultures and local relationships', *Research, Policy and Planning: The Journal of the Social Services Research Group*, 25 (2/3): 129–141.

Radford, L., Corral, S., Bradley, C., Fisher, H., Bassett, C., Howat, N. and Collishaw, S. (2011) 'Child abuse and neglect in the UK today'. London: NSPCC. (Available via: www.sportscoachuk.org/child-abuse-UK)

Sport England (2009) 'High quality community sport for young people: operational standards and guidance for organisations who do not have a recognised club accreditation standard'. London: Sport England.

sports coach UK (2010) *Code of Practice for Sports Coaches* (leaflet). Leeds: Coachwise Ltd/The National Coaching Foundation.

Sports Council Northern Ireland (2006) *Code of Ethics and Good Practice for Children's Sport*. Dublin: The Irish Sports Council.

Vertommen, T., Tolleneer, J., Maebe, G. and De Martelaer, K. (2014) 'Preventing Sexual Abuse and Transgressive Behaviour in Flemish Sport', in Lang, M. and Hartill, M (eds) *Safeguarding, Child Protection and Abuse in Sport: International Perspectives in Research, Policy and Practice*. London: Routledge. ISBN: 978-0-415829-79-3.

## 4.2 Safeguarding/Child Protection Workshops/Training

### sports coach UK Workshops[31]

sports coach UK provides a wide variety of workshops for coaches, including:

- 'Safeguarding and Protecting Children'
- 'Safeguarding and Protecting Children 2: Reflecting on Practice'
- 'Equity in Your Coaching'
- 'How to Coach Disabled People in Sport'
- 'Coaching Children (5–12)'
- 'Positive Behaviour Management in Sport'
- 'How to Coach the Fundamentals of Movement'
- 'Coaching the Young Developing Performer'.

### CPSU Training[32]

The CPSU has developed a range of safeguarding/child protection training and resources, including:

- 'Time to Listen' training for people with designated safeguarding responsibilty at club, county and national level
- 'Safe Sports Events' online tool
- Online safeguarding self-assessment tool
- 'Risk Assessment in Recruitment'
- 'Safeguarding Deaf and Disabled Children in Sport' resources
- 'Case Management' tool and training[33].

The CPSU also delivers bespoke training to sports organisations in response to specific needs and facilitates/contributes to a range of conferences.

### Safeguarding in Sport (CHILDREN 1ST and **sport**scotland) Training[34]

Safeguarding in Sport and **sport**scotland offer a number of workshops which cover the following:

- 'In Safe Hands' workshop – aimed at sports club child protection officers
- Supporting Clubs to Keep Children Safe
- Identifying and Managing Risk
- Recruitment and Selection
- Managing the Disciplinary Process
- Reviewing Child Protection Concerns
- Involving Children in Decision Making
- Child Protection Briefing for Boards.

### Governing Body of Sport Training

A number of governing bodies of sport have developed sport-specific safeguarding/child protection resources, training courses and/or workshops for coaches, staff and volunteers. Contact your governing body for further information.

### County Sports Partnerships (CSPs)

CSPs facilitate or offer access to a number of sports coach UK workshops (see left) for local coaches and volunteers. Contact your local CSP for further information.

### LSCB Training

In some areas, the LSCB provides access to basic multi-agency safeguarding/child protection courses for staff/volunteers in the sports sector. Contact your local LSCB for information.

### NSPCC Training

- The NSPCC provides a range of training courses for a variety of audiences, including regular courses, learning resources and bespoke training. More information can be found on the NSPCC website (www.nspcc.org.uk/what-you-can-do/get-expert-training), by calling 0844-892 1026 or emailing contactus@nspcc.org.uk

---

[31] Visit www.sportscoachuk.org
[32] See Section 4.4 for CPSU contact details.
[33] In development.
**80**
[34] www.children1st.org.uk/what-we-do/our-services/search-our-services/safeguarding-in-sport/training/

## 4.3 sports coach UK Contacts

**sports coach UK**
Chelsea Close
Off Amberley Road
Armley
Leeds LS12 4HP
Tel: 0113-274 4802
Fax: 0113-231 9606
Email: coaching@sportscoachuk.org
Website: www.sportscoachuk.org

Details of all sports coach UK publications are available from:

**1st4sport.com**
Chelsea Close
Off Amberley Road
Armley
Leeds LS12 4HP
Tel: 0113-201 5555
Fax: 0113-231 9606
Email: enquiries@1st4sport.com
Website: www.1st4sport.com

sports coach UK works closely with governing bodies of sport and other Partners to provide a comprehensive service for coaches throughout the UK. This includes an extensive programme of workshops, which have proved valuable to coaches from all types of sports and at every level of experience.

For further details of sports coach UK workshops in your area, please visit the website:
www.sportscoachuk.org

## 4.4 Other Useful Contacts

This section lists a selection of organisations that can provide support and guidance on child protection issues. It is divided into subsections to make it easier to find the organisation(s) you are looking for.

### Confidential Helplines

If this resource has raised personal issues for you, the following organisations will be able to offer confidential help and advice:

- **The Albany Trust**
  (Tel: 020-8767 1827; www.albanytrust.org)
  They offer one-to-one counselling for people who have been sexually abused or suffer from psychological difficulties.

- **ChildLine** (Tel: 0800-1111; www.childline.org.uk)
  Confidential telephone advice for children who are being abused or are at risk – there are a number of ways to contact ChildLine, and more information is available on their website.

- **Child Protection in Sport Unit** (CPSU)
  (Tel: 0116-366 5590; www.thecpsu.org.uk;
  email: cspsu@nspcc.org.uk)
  NSPCC National Training Centre
  3 Gilmour Close
  Beaumont Leys
  Leicester LE4 1EZ
  This serves as a point of contact for sports clubs and individuals who need help and advice with safeguarding and child protection issues in sport. Guidance and downloadable materials are available on the website.

- **Contact NI** (Tel: 0808-808 8000; www.contactni.com)
Counselling service in Northern Ireland.

- **Family Lives**
(Tel: 0808-800 2222; www.familylives.org.uk)
A national charity providing help and support in
various aspects of family life.

- **Local Rape Crisis Centres**
(England and Wales: Tel: 0808-802 9999;
www.rapecrisis.org.uk
Scotland: Tel: 0808-801 0302;
www.rapecrisisscotland.org.uk
Northern Ireland: Tel: 1800-778 888;
www.rcni.ie)
These centres offer help to survivors of abuse.
You will find the number of your local centre in
the telephone directory or on the websites above.

- **Nexus Institute**
(Tel: 028-9032 6803; www.nexusinstitute.org)
Offers counselling for adult survivors of sexual abuse
in Northern Ireland.

- **NSPCC** (Tel: 0808-800 5000; www.nspcc.org.uk)
The NSPCC provides advice and support for
children who have been abused, and for adults or
other children who are concerned that a child has
been abused or is at risk of radicalisation.

- **NSPCC Whistleblowing Advice Line**
(Tel: 0800-028 0285)
Provides free advice for anyone concerned about
how child protection issues are being handled in
their organisation.

- **Parent Line Scotland** (Tel: 0800-028 2233;
email parentlinescotland@children1st.org.uk)
This is a free and confidential helpline for parents.

- **Safeguarding in Sport (CHILDREN 1ST
and sport**scotland**)**
(Tel: 0141-418 5674; www.safeguardinginsport.org.uk)
Safeguarding in Sport operates in Scotland and
works in partnership with the CPSU to promote
consistency and the sharing of good practice across
the UK.

## Home Country Sports Councils

In addition to seeking the advice of the governing body
in your sport, the following organisations will also be
able to offer help and advice:

### Sport England
3rd Floor, Victoria House
Bloomsbury Square
London WC1B 4SE
Tel: 020-7273 1551
Fax: 020-7383 5740
Email: info@sportengland.org
Website: www.sportengland.org

### Sport Northern Ireland
House of Sport
2a Upper Malone Road
Belfast BT9 5LA
Tel: 028-9038 1222
Fax: 028-9068 2757
Email: info@sportni.net
Website: www.sportni.net

### **sport**scotland
Doges
Templeton on the Green
62 Templeton Street
Glasgow G40 1DA
Tel: 0141-534 6500
Fax: 0141-534 6501
Email: **sport**scotland.enquiries@sportscotland.org.uk
Website: www.sportscotland.org.uk

### Sport Wales
Sophia Gardens
Cardiff CF11 9SW
Tel: 0845-045 0904
Fax: 0845-846 0014
Email: info@sportwales.org.uk
Website: www.sportwales.org.uk

### UK Sport
40 Bernard Street
London WC1N 1ST
Tel: 020-7211 5100
Fax: 020-7211 5246
Email: info@uksport.gov.uk
Website: www.uksport.gov.uk

## Other Organisations

### AccessNI
PO Box 1085
Belfast BT5 9BD
Tel: 0300-200 7888
Email: accessni@ani.x.gsi.gov.uk
Website: www.accessni.gov.uk

### Central Registered Body in Scotland
Jubilee House
Forthside Way
Stirling FK8 1QZ
Tel: 01786-849 777
Fax: 01786-849 767
Email: info@crbs.org.uk
Website: www.crbs.org.uk

### CHILDREN 1ST
83 Whitehouse Loan
Edinburgh EH9 1AT
Tel: 0131-446 2300
Fax: 0131-446 2339
Email: info@children1st.org.uk
Website: www.children1st.org.uk

### Department of Health, Social Services and Public Safety Northern Ireland
Castle Buildings
Stormont
Belfast BT4 3SJ
Tel: 028-9052 0416/028-9052 2951
Email: childp@dhsspsni.gov.uk
Website: www.dhsspsni.gov.uk

### Disclosure and Barring Service
For any disclosure application queries:
PO Box 110
Liverpool L69 3EF
Tel: 0870-9090 811
Website: www.homeoffice.gov.uk/dbs

For any barring referrals and safeguarding matters:
PO Box 181
Darlington DL1 9FA
Tel: 01325-953 795

For all freedom of information, data protection and subject access requests, enquiries should be addressed to the relevant department at this address:
PO Box 165
Liverpool L69 3JD

### Disclosure Scotland
PO Box 250
Glasgow G51 1YU
Tel: 0870-609 6006
Fax: 0870-609 6996
Email: info@disclosurescotland.co.uk
Website: www.disclosurescotland.co.uk

### NSPCC
Weston House
42 Curtain Road
London EC2A 3NH
Tel: 020-7825 2505
Email: help@nspcc.org.uk
Website: www.nspcc.org.uk

### Safeguarding Board for Northern Ireland
18 Ormeau Road
Belfast BT2 8HS
Tel: 028-9031 1611
Email: sbnisupport@hscni.net
Website: www.safeguardingni.org

## Feedback – Activity 1

### Scenario 1

Although it is natural for children to get upset if they are given negative feedback, you should never give feedback that is intended to cause upset or humiliation in front of others. Instead, it is important to learn how to provide constructive feedback, and to ensure this is not overheard by other competitors or spectators. This approach will allow children to both acknowledge their strengths and consider how they could improve their performance in future matches.

### Scenario 2

If a coach attempts to lay blame in this way, he is acting in an unprofessional manner. If Scott is overweight, the coach should talk to Scott and his parents about what help he might need instead of raising this in public, leading to embarrassment and making him feel like a victim in front of his fellow team members. This may result in Scott giving up the sport with memories of a negative experience and may cause him emotional harm.

### Scenario 3

This is a difficult situation, but no child should be penalised because of their religious beliefs. If the coach maintains this attitude, the children concerned may decide to drop out of the team and the coach may be considered a bully. Under the terms of the Children Act 1989 and the Children (Scotland) Act 1995, all children have the right to be consulted about what they want to do. This is also included within most organisational equity and inclusion policies and practice.

### Scenario 4

In this case, Claire's mother's personal beliefs mean she will not allow her daughter to take part in a mixed class. Deciding that an excellent alternative would be to allow Claire to swim with a girls-only class, she has booked this class in advance. It is not until she arrives at the swimming pool that Claire discovers she cannot attend the class on offer. The coach should have advised Claire's mother of changes prior to the class being held to provide a choice about whether or not Claire can participate.

### Scenario 5

It is not acceptable for the instructor to deny this child the opportunity to participate in sessions without seeking to understand the implications of the reported learning disability in the context of the planned activity. The instructor should talk to the mother and child about what (if any) steps may need to be taken to accommodate the boy, and what support or advice the instructor may require from the mother. Disabled children can often be fully included in activities with little or no significant adaptations to activity rules or equipment. Focus on what a child can do, rather than what he/she cannot.

## Feedback – Activity 2

### Physical contact

It is sometimes appropriate and necessary to have direct physical contact with children in order to develop their skills in a safe environment. There is growing concern being expressed about what is and is not permissible in the area of physical contact with children and young people in sport. The priority for the coach and child is the application of safe and appropriate coaching methods.

There have also been instances where some coaches and other adults who are motivated to harm and abuse children and young people have done so by falsely claiming that their behaviours were legitimate teaching, coaching or caring practices.

Many governing bodies of sport provide useful guidance to their coaches on this issue, which reflects the specific requirements of their sport and is proportionate in relation to their responsibility to promote a safe and enjoyable environment for all participants. There is also further general guidance on the CPSU website.

### Training practices

In some sports, you may need to explain training practices in detail so everyone involved in the coaching process understands exactly why and when factors relating to intensity, duration, nutrition or treatment are important.

### Communication

Always consider the age and abilities of all the children you are working with in order to establish the most effective communication method. This may simply involve amending your technical terminology (you may need to simplify the language used), but could also mean adapting your approach to reflect the needs of children with a particular impairment/disability (for example a deaf child).

You should try to ensure the language and communication methods you use does not confuse children; it should not be a barrier to their understanding and enjoyment of sport.

## Player welfare

As someone with regular responsibility for young people, you are more likely to spot issues that concern you about their welfare, including medical, training and personal issues. Where possible, it is important that you involve the child and their parents in discussions to resolve these issues. However, if this would place the child at immediate risk, such as when a child is in need of urgent medical attention, it is important that the child's welfare is of paramount concern and there is no delay in obtaining assistance or reporting concerns.

## Coaching services

You should discuss and agree on experts or organisations that can offer appropriate further services with the child and/or parents. Always inform the child and/or parents of any potential costs involved. You should clarify the boundary of your role between giving advice as a coach and providing medical/therapeutic advice/treatment.

## Feedback – Activity 3

You may have listed some or all of the following issues:

- health
- safety
- insurance
- risk assessment
- paperwork (including session register, session plan, training programme)
- incident forms
- information for parents
- consent checks
- phone numbers (parents, other key club members such as the club welfare officer)
- assessment of particular needs of disabled participants
- professional qualifications
- being a role model
- standards of dress and behaviour
- secure storage of information about children
- photography
- arrangements for contacting children (email, texting, phone call)
- references
- links with other coaches and professionals
- driving insurance
- first aid.

## Feedback - Activity 4

### Good practice involves seeking support when you need it.

As a coach, you should never feel you are alone – you should feel able to seek help, advice or support whenever it may help you deal with an issue.

Your diagram may have included some, or all, of the following groups of people. You may like to use the spaces provided below to note the names, telephone numbers and email addresses of specific people in your club or local area to whom you may turn for help and support.

| People Who May Help | Name(s) | Telephone | Email |
|---|---|---|---|
| Club welfare/child protection officer | | | |
| County welfare/child protection officer | | | |
| Other coaches in your club | | | |
| Other coaches in your local area | | | |
| Friends | | | |
| Your line manager | | | |
| Head coach | | | |
| Development officer/sports development officer | | | |
| County development officer | | | |
| Regional organiser | | | |
| Governing body of sport | | | |
| Governing body of sport safeguarding lead officer | | | |
| Local leisure authority | | | |
| Club committee | | | |
| Club employees/caretaker/ groundsperson | | | |
| Parents | | | |
| Young people in your club | | | |
| Doctor/dentist | | | |
| Children's services | | | |
| Emergency services (eg fire, police, ambulance) | | | |
| Insurance company | | | |

## Feedback - Activity 6

The committee at Parkgate Sports Club has made every effort to provide a high quality programme of activities for children that meets standards of good practice.

The many examples of good practice demonstrated in the scenario should contribute to the provision of a positive sporting environment for children.
These include:

- providing good club facilities (eg drinking water, telephone, security lighting, overnight security guard)
- not only having a club committee, but having one that is committed to supporting staff, meeting customer needs and providing a safe, secure environment
- reviewing previous activities to identify examples of good practice and areas for improvement
- providing training for committee members and staff, including the introduction of the code of practice
- achieving Clubmark accreditation, which can give parents confidence in the quality of the club
- having a designated coaching officer responsible for planning the club's programme of activities
- providing activities for different age groups
- allocating roles and responsibilities to specific staff
- having formal recruitment and induction procedures (including appropriate checks)
- keeping records of children attending the club
- providing orientation sessions for children and their parents
- making every effort to be equitable and cater for all children, including those with specific needs
- considering the communication, personal care and other needs of disabled children
- carrying out risk assessments of activities, resources and equipment
- controlling the arrival and departure of people at the club and keeping a register of attendance
- obtaining and acting on customer feedback.

## Feedback - Activity 7

This is a very common situation. Young or inexperienced players may often feel that the only way to win is to copy poor behaviour they have seen elsewhere. In this example, the players on the coach's team felt they were not going to win without resorting to desperate measures – even though they could be considered to be cheating. They felt that if they 'cheated', they would score goals. They did not associate the concept of 'fair play' with their present situation, but were only focused on the idea of winning.

## Feedback - Activity 9

All the scenarios in this activity are examples of situations in which things are not quite right and where it is important to refer back to your code of practice and organisational guidelines. As a coach, it is important to demonstrate exemplary behaviour at all times in order to safeguard athletes and reduce the likelihood of an allegation being made.

Poor practice can be harmful for participants, coaches and the club. It provides a negative model of behaviour and attitude for others, and may lead to misconceptions about the motivation and intent of those involved. It may contribute to creating an environment in which other inappropriate behaviour is accepted or can flourish. Most seriously, poor practice may be part of the grooming process (see page 39) employed by an individual who is motivated to abuse a child, or may escalate into other abusive behaviour.

Sound recruitment processes, the application of codes of practice, and prompt reporting of, and responses to, concerns can all contribute to eradicating poor practice and reducing these associated risks.

## Feedback - Activity 10

A whole range of emotions may be experienced when faced with possible child abuse. There can sometimes be a self-protective impulse to deny the reality and implications of child abuse. Many people feel emotions such as anger, shock and dismay, perhaps followed by feelings of sadness, sympathy or powerlessness. These feelings are very natural, and it is important to recognise and acknowledge how they may impact on your ability to respond appropriately.

## Feedback - Activity 11

You may have found that some of the examples were quite easy to respond to (eg a teacher having sexual intercourse with a child is clearly illegal, unacceptable and constitutes abusive behaviour). Some are also covered by legislation (eg the age of consent for sexual intercourse is 16 years in England, Wales, Northern Ireland and Scotland). There is an important distinction between the role of a coach and that of a PE teacher. It is illegal for a teacher to have a sexual relationship with a young person under the age of 18 who they are teaching, whereas this is considered poor practice for a coach (and is against the code of practice for most governing bodies of sport), but is not against the law.

You will probably have found others more difficult and found yourself saying, 'It would depend on...' or, 'I would need to know more about...'. Some of these would not constitute child abuse (eg because of the age of the participant), nor would they contravene legislation. However, they may contravene an ethical code of practice for coaches and others involved in children's sport (eg a coach having a sexual relationship with a 16-year-old participant may constitute an abuse of trust and thus warrant disciplinary action).

Scenario 15 suggests that young people in the group may be being groomed, by a person in a position of trust, in radical ideologies. Adults looking to influence young people in this way are abusing their position and relationship with young people in a similar way to those who may groom young people for sexual activity. Grooming of this nature is not limited to any single group in society and abusers have been known to target both children, often disenfranchised young men, and some adults at risk. This is abuse and if you have concerns that a young person is being groomed in radical ideologies you must inform the police. The young person will be offered considerable support by the police and usually considered a victim of abuse rather than a criminal. The prevention of radicalisation is now considered a serious form of abuse children may be at risk from by adults in a position of trust, friends or even by family members. As such local authorities, educational institutions and some sports organisations now offer training to adults in a position of trust on preventing the radicalisation of young people.

## Feedback – Activity 12

1  **False**

Most children who are affected by abuse are abused by adults they know and trust.

2  **False**

Women also sexually abuse children, although far less often than men.

Those who sexually abuse children could be family members or friends, neighbours or babysitters – many hold responsible positions in society. Some people who abuse children also have adult sexual relationships and are not solely, or even mainly, sexually interested in children. Abusers come from all classes, ethnic and religious backgrounds and may be homosexual or heterosexual. Most sexual abusers are men, but some are women. In addition, 23–40% of all alleged sexual abuse of children and young people is perpetrated by other young people, mainly adolescents[35].

3  **False**

Deaf and disabled children are up to four times as likely to be abused as non-disabled children. One study in 2000 found that 31% of disabled children had been abused compared with a prevalence of 9% in the non-disabled population[36]. Disabled children are more vulnerable to abuse due to a range of factors, such as being more likely to be dependent on practical assistance in daily living, including intimate care; sometimes less able to tell anyone or remove themselves from abusive situations; and less likely to be believed.

4  **False**

A study of the experiences of children within sport found that, in general, the ratios were roughly equal. However, in the case of sexual harassment, overall, girls were more likely to be abused than boys[37].

5  **False**

Child abuse is unacceptable in all cultures, and there is no government or society that sanctions it. However, there are sometimes differences in how child abuse is defined, and what may be considered acceptable standards of behaviour towards, and care of, children. Assumptions (particularly those based on stereotypes) about what may be considered acceptable by different groups should not affect a decision to record and report concerns about children's welfare. All residents of the UK must comply with UK legislation regarding children's safeguarding and protection.

[35] Lovell, E. (2002) 'Children and young people who display sexually harmful behaviour'. London: NSPCC.
[36] Sullivan, P.M. and Knutson, J.F. (2000) 'Maltreatment and disabilities: a population-based epidemiological study', *Child Abuse and Neglect*, 24 (10): 1257–1273.
[37] Alexander, K., Stafford, A. and Lewis, R. (2011) *The Experiences of Children Participating in Organised Sport in the UK*. Edinburgh: The University of Edinburgh/NSPCC Centre for UK-wide Learning in Child Protection. ISBN: 978-1-908055-04-0.

## 6 **False**

Children's services will only take action to remove children when there is a risk of significant harm and if the child is in real danger of further abuse. They work in partnership with parents, to offer as much support as possible. In the minority of cases where it is deemed too unsafe for a child to remain with their parents, consideration is given to placing the child within the wider family network, with fostering or residential care used as a last resort. The decision is always made by a court except in emergency situations where the police have special powers.

## 7 **False**

All abuse is harmful. If untreated, the effects of abuse on children can be devastating and may continue into adulthood. The resilience of individual children to abuse is based on a complex combination of personal factors and circumstances (including the support received following disclosure). Assumptions about the impact of abuse on a child, particularly those based on a judgement about the nature or apparent seriousness of their experiences, should be avoided.

## 8 **False**

Research in 2011 found worrying levels of emotionally harmful treatment and unacceptable levels of sexual harassment in sport. It also found that while experience of harm occurs at every level of sport, there is a tendency for it to increase with level of participation[38].

More recently research showed that significant numbers of children and young people experienced all forms of abuse within sport, with certain groups (disabled, talented and LGBT young people) reporting the highest levels of harm.[39]

## 9 **True**

Some children wrongly feel responsible for their abuse and may want to protect the abuser by denying their experiences. Very often, children have been threatened with something bad happening if they tell anyone, which means it takes considerable courage for them to disclose their abuse. This makes it vital that children are listened to and taken seriously. Children rarely lie about abuse. The common perception that many children invent

allegations of abuse is not supported by the experiences of childcare professionals. In fact, many children who experience abuse do not tell anyone, and recent research has found that more than one in five children aged 11–17 (22.9%) who were physically hurt by a parent did not tell anyone else about it[40].

## 10 **False**

Research from 2011 suggests that peer on peer is the most prevalent form of abuse in a sporting context, with 69% of reported cases being of this nature[41].

## Feedback – Activity 14

There may be potential child welfare concerns that can or do arise in your sport. For example, the physical risk of some contact sports may need to be anticipated and managed. Often, the relevant governing body of sport has acknowledged and addressed these issues, usually by issuing specific good-practice guidance for coaches and participants. It may be helpful for you to contact your governing body of sport to raise any issues or concerns you have identified, and access any existing guidance that will assist in dealing with these situations. The CPSU and CHILDREN 1ST also offer advice and guidance on a range of specific issues through their respective websites: www.thecpsu.org.uk and www.safeguardinginsport.org.uk

## Feedback – Activity 15

Physical contact can be used to explain sporting techniques (eg how to hold a javelin) or prevent harm to children. However, clear guidelines about when physical contact is appropriate will ensure coaches, children, parents and others understand what is acceptable and when there is cause for concern.

## Feedback – Activity 17

### Scenario 1

Some children have a strong desire to maintain privacy. In this case, the child may have a skin condition that other children could see and potentially make fun of, she could be self-conscious about her body and undressing in public, or there may be religious reasons why she would prefer to remain covered. By avoiding getting changed in public, this child ensures the condition

[38] Alexander, K., Stafford, A. and Lewis, R. (2011) *The Experiences of Children Participating in Organised Sport in the UK*. Edinburgh: The University of Edinburgh/NSPCC Centre for UK-wide Learning in Child Protection. ISBN: 978-1-908055-04-0.

[39] Vertommen, T., Tolleneer, J., Maebe, G. and De Martelaer, K. (2014) 'Preventing Sexual Abuse and Transgressive Behaviour in Flemish Sport', in Lang, M. and Hartill, M (eds) *Safeguarding, Child Protection and Abuse in Sport: International Perspectives in Research, Policy and Practice*. London: Routledge. ISBN: 978-0-415829-79-3.

[40] Radford, L., Corral, S., Bradley, C., Fisher, H., Bassett, C., Howat, N. and Collishaw, S. (2011) 'Child abuse and neglect in the UK today'. London: NSPCC.

[41] Alexander, K., Stafford, A. and Lewis, R. (2011) *The Experiences of Children Participating in Organised Sport in the UK*. Edinburgh: The University of Edinburgh/NSPCC Centre for UK-wide Learning in Child Protection. ISBN: 978-1-908055-04-0.

remains a secret and maintains the appearance that she is the same as everyone else. The coach may want to address this with the girl herself to acknowledge the concerns and ask her about it. Alternatively, they might want to raise this with her parents to discuss the issue.

## Scenario 2

It is not clear from this scenario whether the young woman is upset due to her difficulties in understanding or doing the activity, due to other concerns or due to bullying by other children. However, what is evident is that the coach has had difficulty in supervising all the children and would benefit from additional support to manage this situation. The coach might want to ask the young woman why she is upset and/or raise this with her mother. The coach might also consider this with their colleagues and arrange additional support with the group.

## Scenario 3

This scenario exposes players to the unknown. Straight away, several children will feel inadequate and reluctant to play with older players because they don't want to look silly. For other children, this will be a challenge and an adventure. Discussion with the players to help decision making would be helpful in this situation.

## Feedback – Activity 18

The list you have compiled may cover some or all of the following signs:

- unexplained bruising or injuries
- sexually explicit actions or language
- changes in behaviour or mood
- something a child has said
- a change observed over a long period of time (eg weight loss, increasingly dirty or unkempt).

All these factors are important, and children may often suffer from more than one form of abuse. For example, a child who is repeatedly smacked for minor misdemeanours may also experience emotional abuse because they feel frightened, anxious or worthless.

> **Remember!**
>
> Evidence of a combination or repetition of signs over time should alert you to possible problems, not just one bruise.

## Feedback – Activity 19

This is a very difficult situation. Concerns include the following:

- Practical issues – Sarah's father may not be able to give her practical support through providing food, drink and a safe environment. You do not know the extent of Sarah's disability or adaptations within the home, but Sarah may have additional needs that her father is not able to provide in his current state (eg leaving the house quickly in the case of a fire).

- Emotional support – there may also be concerns about the father's lack of support for Sarah, and the possibility of alcohol abuse and depression. However, it is not your role to diagnose problems but to report concerns appropriately.

- The possible lack of basic care and emotional support could be considered as neglect.

- It is important that Sarah's welfare and safety remain your primary concern, and that action is taken to address the identified concerns. Sarah may want to protect her father and not be fully aware of the risks to which she is exposed. Her father may initially be angry at what could be perceived as interference. However, both may also be relieved that someone is recognising their difficulties and responding to these.

### What happened?

Sarah was struggling to manage her own feelings and look after herself alongside her concern for her father. Her father had been drinking heavily for several months, but this had got worse over the last few weeks and he has been neglecting practical care of Sarah as well as being unavailable for her and unable to provide emotional support.

## Feedback – Activity 20

Minor cuts, bruises and soft tissue injuries (eg strains and tears) are quite common in some sports. The areas where bruising is most likely to occur are the bony parts of the body (eg elbows, knees, shins or forehead).

**Remember!**

You should be aware of children's injuries or bruising that can only be caused non-accidentally. These will often be part of a recurring pattern, sometimes appearing regularly (eg after a weekend). An important indicator of physical abuse is where bruises or injuries are:

- unexplained

- untreated

- inadequately treated (or where there are delays to treatment)

- on parts of the body where accidental injuries are unlikely (eg on the cheeks or thighs).

Bruising may be more or less noticeable on children with different skin tones or from different racial groups. You need to be alert to the following **physical signs**:

- unexplained bruising, marks or injuries on any part of the body

- bruises that reflect hand marks or fingertips (from slapping, grabbing, pinching)

- burns in distinctive shapes

- broken bones

- scalds.

Physical abuse may not always be apparent from bruises, fractures or physical signs. **Behavioural signs**, particularly when there are changes in behaviour, can also indicate that abuse is happening. This might be evident in the following behaviours:

- fear of parents being contacted

- aggressive behaviour or severe temper outbursts

- running away

- fear of going home (eg after training sessions)

- flinching when approached or touched

- reluctance to get changed for sport

- covering arms and legs even when hot (eg during hard physical activity or in hot weather)

- withdrawn behaviour.

Remember that any one indicator needs to be seen within a pattern of concerns as other explanations for behaviour are also possible.

## Feedback – Activity 21

It would appear from what the boys are saying that their father gets involved in their boxing practice. They do not appear to be aware of the dangers of punching to the head area, and Jim's comment would indicate that his father may have punched his head. The risks include physical injury of Ben by Jim, of either boy by their father, and the possibility that this is an indicator of further abuse or bullying.

### What happened?

The coach raised his concerns with the club welfare officer, who spoke with Ben and Jim's parents. Their father was angry about his behaviour being challenged and said he was trying to get involved in the children's activities. However, on further discussion with their mother, it appeared that their father liked to 'fight' with the boys after a stressful day at work and sometimes used them to vent his frustrations, leading to the occasional mark or bruise. Recently, this had been happening more, due to additional work pressures. The club welfare officer expressed her concerns and called children's services to discuss the matter further. A social worker visited the family, and it was agreed to do some work with the parents to talk about how they managed the pressures on them and to increase their awareness of the dangers of physical abuse. Following this, the father became involved in the club as a volunteer where he was provided with further training about appropriate boxing techniques for children, and started to box himself as a stress-reduction technique.

## Feedback – Activity 23

Children with disabilities may be more vulnerable to abuse. It is possible Peter has targeted Linda for abuse due to this vulnerability. Linda appears confused about what behaviour is appropriate, indicating some inappropriate behaviour at home, and also speaks of her dislike for Peter, accompanied by fear of giving further information.

It is important to take these concerns seriously, placing clear boundaries around appropriate touch while supporting Linda and giving her time to talk about concerns. Instead of questioning Linda, space should be provided for her to confide concerns and the pattern of concerns passed on to the club welfare officer. Further investigations would be undertaken by trained professionals, such as social workers and police officers, if appropriate.

### What happened?

After a long conversation about her worries, Linda eventually confided that Peter had 'snogged' her and made her touch his genital area. He told her this is what people who like each other do. The coach spoke to the club welfare officer, who informed children's services. The police and children's services talked to Linda, who told them what was happening. Peter denied the allegation, and Linda's mother also initially did not believe this, but it was eventually agreed that Peter would leave the family home. Children's services referred Linda and her mother to a local family centre, which worked with them both to address the traumatic effect of what happened, and to support Linda during the police's ongoing investigation.

## Feedback – Activity 24

Children who are talented and gifted are at increased risk of abuse due to the additional expectations upon them and closer relationships with coaches. George's insulting remarks to Huan are both abusive and likely to be in breach of his code of practice. They are also having the effect of undermining rather than improving her behaviour. There are also issues around George providing one-to-one coaching for Huan – this places them both in a vulnerable position and is also likely to be against organisational procedures. Huan is particularly vulnerable as English is not her first language, and she is likely to be less familiar with British cultural expectations. She will find it more difficult to identify and challenge inappropriate behaviour.

Responding to concerns about a colleague's behaviour is very difficult, particularly if you know the person well, and the consequences of reporting allegations may have far-reaching effects. Equally, it is important to remember that failing to report a colleague may also have far-reaching effects for this child and perhaps others. Poor practice cannot go unchallenged, and it may be part of a more serious problem of abuse, which places children at serious risk.

### What happened?

In this situation, George's behaviour was reported to the gymnastics club's welfare officer. It transpired that this was not the first occasion on which concerns had been expressed about his behaviour, and the matter was taken seriously and acted upon immediately. Huan's parents were informed. The club welfare officer sought advice from the governing body of sport, and it was agreed that George should undertake further training. During this period, George's coaching was covered by a colleague. The issue also led to a decision to give further training to all coaches at the club around appropriate training for talented gymnasts to help them develop their skills in a supportive environment.

## Feedback – Activity 26

If you work in a club that has clear guidelines and procedures to follow when abuse is suspected, and a designated person to whom you can report your concerns (usually the head teacher, club welfare officer, coach, most senior person), they should be able to assist with completing this form or refer you to the child protection procedures.

If your club either does not currently have any clear procedures or, if it does, you are unaware of them, seek guidance from your employer (or, if you work in a voluntary capacity, the person responsible for your work) or contact your governing body of sport.

If you are self-employed or a volunteer and work with children at a private venue (eg a gym club in the village hall, athletics session at a college track, football session on the church field, tennis lesson on a friend's private court), there may not be anyone to whom you can report your concerns. If you are in this situation, if there is no one else available or if you are the most senior person, **you will have to take responsibility for taking the next step**. You will need to familiarise yourself with the recommended guidelines and draw up your own code of practice.

Whether you are part of a public, private or voluntary body, you have a duty of care (see Appendix C) for the children with whom you work. This means every organisation should have a policy that clearly states that it is the duty of all those employed or involved to take steps to ensure the safety, and prevent the physical, sexual or emotional abuse, of children with whom they come into contact.

## Feedback – Activity 27

Both of these scenarios occur in many sporting settings. However, in the kind of set-up in Case Study 1, there are a number of risks that are more effectively prevented in Case Study 2. Fortunately, clubs organised on an informal basis, like this one, often develop and adopt the more formal structure of the club described in Case Study 2.

| Case Study 1 | Case Study 2 |
|---|---|
| Absence of information available for parents about the club set-up, rules, regulations, coaches, schedules etc. | Clear information sent to parents at the outset. |
| Lack of transparency around regulations for trips, travel, coach:player ratios and parental permission. | Clear forms to obtain parental permission supported by information about regulations and procedures. |
| Young coaches do not appear to be supervised or supported – in this case, they are also responsible for transport. | Transparent arrangements for the support, training and supervision of younger coaches. |
| Online settings do not have built-in safeguards, with risks of being open to the downloading of unchecked materials, including photographs and information about the coaches. Younger club members are encouraged to join up. | Clear rules on the use of online settings/social media, which cover membership and use of the settings, making them more safe environments. |

Given the choice, the good practice illustrated in Case Study 2 should be the way forward. Parents have the right to make these choices for their children. In turn, coaches have the opportunity to provide choices that make sport safe for children.

## Feedback – Activity 28

Every club should ensure all reasonable steps are taken to prevent unsuitable people, whether paid or unpaid, from working with children.

The manager of this club made a concerted effort to recruit suitable staff. Examples of good practice include:

- seeking approval from the club committee to recruit extra staff – it is important the committee is kept aware of all club activities

- ensuring the advert contains relevant information about the club and the posts available – this will help to attract the right kind of people

- carrying out a formal application process and asking for a reference

- conducting formal interviews to assess the suitability of the candidates

- making all candidates aware of what will be expected of them

- providing successful candidates with a formal induction to the club and regular feedback on their progress.

In addition to the above, the manager could have:

- asked applicants for two written references instead of just one – including one from an employer or, in the case of the students, a tutor from the local college

- selected applicants with some or all of the following attributes: first aid training; child protection training; coaching experience; and skill updates

- implemented formal monitoring and appraisal procedures for all club staff, particularly the new recruits.

If the posts were in 'regulated activity'[42] (ie they were to be responsible for, and regularly in contact with, children), the manager could also have asked applicants to complete a self-declaration form and required an enhanced level DBS disclosure.

## Feedback – Activity 29

The extracts from the club's records all describe incidents that required a person's response, and which, if left, could have become far more serious and placed children in danger of physical, emotional and sexual abuse or neglect.

Fortunately, the club in question had procedures in place to minimise any damaging or harmful effects in the event of a situation arising in which abuse could occur.

Further ongoing actions could include:

- minimising opportunities for an adult to be left alone with a single child

- providing opportunities for coaches to talk to parents about the expected standards of behaviour of young participants

- introducing clear guidelines and procedures for transporting children, for away and overnight trips, and for photography

- arranging for coaches to meet children with their parents present

- coaches encouraging parents to attend training sessions and support competitions

- carrying out random checks on coaching practice

- carrying out routine risk assessments of the premises and ensuring recommendations are acted on swiftly by the club committee

- encouraging parents to take greater responsibility for ensuring the safety of their child

- introducing a system enabling children with concerns to talk to an independent person outside the club – this person should be given clear written guidelines on the action to take if abuse is disclosed or suspected

- ensuring agreed procedures for protecting children apply to all staff (whether paid or voluntary, full- or part-time, permanent or temporary). This should include:

  - ensuring all staff have clear roles and responsibilities

  - issuing guidelines on the action to take if abuse is disclosed or suspected

  - implementing a supervision and appraisal system that monitors roles and relationships, and observes coaching practice.

Measures such as these not only protect the children, but also protect coaches by reducing the likelihood of accusations of improper behaviour being made.

---

[42] Regulated activity includes activities such as teaching, training, care, supervision, advice, treatment and transportation of children or vulnerable adults. Individuals engaging in those activities must be carrying them out either frequently (once per week or more) or intensively (four or more days in a 30-day period, or overnight). It also includes activities that take place in certain settings, such as a school. For further information, see www.homeoffice.gov.uk

## Safe Recruitment and Selection Procedures

The majority of people who want to work or volunteer with children within sport are well motivated, and without them, sports clubs could not operate. Unfortunately, some individuals will try to use sports clubs and events to gain access to children for inappropriate motives. Having safe recruitment and selection procedures in place will help deter and screen out unsuitable individuals from your club or event.

The same procedures should be adopted whether staff are paid or unpaid, full- or part-time.

The club should ensure effective recruitment and selection procedures by:

• providing a clear job/role description for each post, which describes the full range of duties the role will involve, and a person specification that describes the type of skills and attributes you require the post-holder to have

• advertising paid jobs/volunteer roles through various methods and including an indication that the post involves working with children and (if appropriate) a criminal records check will be undertaken

• ensuring any person applying for a post within a club or for an event completes the club's standard application form, which should include a section allowing the individual to self-declare any convictions or relevant information and confirming their consent for a criminal records check to be undertaken (where this is appropriate for the post)

• obtaining two written references; these should preferably include their last employer or person who deployed them, and someone who can comment on their previous work with children; ideally, referees should be contacted directly

• having a process in place to risk assess information returned from any of the above sources and assist with decision making, with training provided for the person/people responsible for these decisions

• ensuring staff or volunteers undertake an interview or have a meeting with at least two representatives of the club where there is the opportunity to check out any gaps in the application form and ensure the applicant has the ability and commitment to meet the standards required to put the child protection policy into practice

• setting a probationary/trial period (usually six months); every new post should be reviewed within an agreed period of time

• ensuring all appointments are made by more than one person

• ensuring all new recruits go through an induction process as soon as possible so they are familiar with the club or event's safeguarding policies and procedures and the responsibilities of the post

• ensuring all new recruits are familiar with and sign up to the club's constitution and rules and any guidelines, codes of behaviour, regulations and policies of the club, sport or event

• ensuring all new recruits register as a member of the club if not already a member

• ensuring all new recruits have either recently undertaken appropriate safeguarding training or arrange for this to take place.

## Disclosure and Barring Service, AccessNI, and Disclosure Scotland Checks

The DBS, AccessNI and Disclosure Scotland were set up by the Home Office and Scottish Executive respectively to improve access to criminal records checks for organisations making decisions about the employment and deployment of staff and volunteers whose role involves responsibility for, or contact with, children and/or vulnerable adults. In particular, it contributes to the safeguarding and protection of children and vulnerable adults from those who may represent a risk to them. Criminal records and other safeguarding checks may be managed through the governing body of sport or an external organisation.

### Disclosures

A disclosure is a document containing impartial and confidential criminal history information held by the police and government departments, which can be used by employers to make safer recruitment decisions.

### Scotland

In February 2011, the Scottish Government introduced a new membership scheme to replace and improve on the current disclosure arrangements for people who work with vulnerable groups, called the Protecting Vulnerable Groups (PVG) Scheme. The PVG Scheme is managed and delivered by Disclosure Scotland, which makes decisions about who should be barred from working with vulnerable groups. Anyone can apply for a basic disclosure in their own name. This covers criminal records information. For most other types of regulated work with children or protected adults, the PVG Scheme is the most appropriate check. 'Regulated work' is the term used by the Protection of Vulnerable Groups (Scotland) Act 2007 to define the types of work barred individuals must not do, and for which PVG Scheme membership is available. This check includes details of criminal records, information about a person's inclusion on barred lists, and other relevant information held by a local police force or government body.

For more information, contact Disclosure Scotland: www.disclosurescotland.org.uk

### England, Wales and Northern Ireland

The Safeguarding Vulnerable Groups Act 2006 and Protection of Freedoms Act 2012 made changes to the arrangements for criminal records checks in England, Wales and Northern Ireland. The DBS was formed on 1 December 2012 when the Criminal Records Bureau (CRB) and the Independent Safeguarding Authority merged into one agency to manage these checks. Within set criteria, the decision about the eligibility of a particular role or post for a DBS check remains the responsibility of the employing body, with guidance from the DBS.

There are two types of DBS check:

1  Standard checks – these checks provide information held on the Police National Computer (PNC), including convictions, cautions, reprimands and warnings in England and Wales, and most of the relevant convictions in Scotland and Northern Ireland may also be included.

2  Enhanced checks – in addition to the information held on the PNC, enhanced checks also provide information held by local police forces and other agencies, relating to relevant non-conviction information. For roles involving regular responsibility for children and young people, organisations are strongly advised to require enhanced level DBS checks. For those roles in 'regulated activity', this will also include a check against the list of individuals barred from working with children and/or vulnerable adults. Regulated activity includes activities such as teaching, training, care, supervision, advice, treatment and transportation of children or vulnerable adults. Individuals engaging in those activities must be carrying them out either frequently (once per week or more) or intensively (four or more days in a 30-day period, or overnight).

The DBS's role is to help prevent unsuitable people from working with vulnerable groups, including children. It maintains a list of individuals barred from engaging in regulated activity with children and of those barred from engaging in regulated activity with vulnerable adults. Organisations are legally required to refer details of individuals considered to represent a risk to children or vulnerable adults to the DBS for consideration for being placed on one of the two barred lists.

For more information, contact the DBS: www.gov.uk/government/organisations/disclosure-and-barring-service

If a club knowingly appoints a person who is banned from working with children, it will be committing a criminal offence, as will the individual by applying for a role that involves working with children. Should a club dismiss an individual following concerns about abuse of children, this information should be passed to the DBS (England and Wales), AccessNI (Northern Ireland) or Disclosure Scotland (Scotland).

The National Occupational Standards for Coaching, Teaching and Instructing (NOS for CTI) are based on a number of competences associated with planning, delivering and evaluating coaching sessions and programmes. The standards are used as part of governing bodies of sport's coach education awards and as the definition of competence for National/Scottish Vocational Qualifications (N/SVQs) in coaching, teaching and instructing. N/SVQs at Levels 2 and 3 are available in a number of sports. sports coach UK has developed its coach development programme around these standards. Its workshops and resources aim to provide the underpinning knowledge for coaches who wish to meet the competences of the standards. They also give coaches guidelines on how to apply this knowledge to their coaching practice.

*Safeguarding and Protecting Children: A Guide for Sportspeople* has been designed to support the following unit of the Level 2/3 NOS:

**Unit C36 Support the protection of children from abuse**

C36.1 Report signs of possible abuse

C36.2 Respond to a child's disclosure of abuse

For further information about the NOS for CTI at Levels 2 and 3, contact SkillsActive at the address on page 83.

# Contents

## England

## Northern Ireland

## Scotland

## Wales

## CPSU Guidance: Duty of Care

## England

### Every Child Matters: Change for Children

The Every Child Matters (ECM) government strategy and subsequent Children Act raised the degree of accountability, especially at senior management level and in all organisations working with children and families, for safeguarding children. The aim for every child, whatever their background or circumstances, was for them to have the support they need to:

- be healthy
- stay safe
- enjoy and achieve
- make a positive contribution
- achieve economic well-being.

This was to be achieved through a variety of organisations involved in providing services to children – from hospitals and schools, to police and voluntary groups – working together.

The ECM publication has been archived but is still available for reference use via: www.sportscoachuk.org/ecm

It should not be considered to reflect current government policy or guidance.

### Working Together to Safeguard Children (Revised 2015)

*Working Together to Safeguard Children* is a key guidance document for all organisations providing services for, or working with, children and young people. It sets out how organisations and individuals should work together to safeguard and promote the welfare of children.

In 2012, the government consulted on its proposals to substantially revise the *Working Together to Safeguard Children* guidance, substantially reducing this and containing it in three separate draft documents:

1   Working Together to Safeguard Children – guidance on what organisations working with children must do to safeguard and promote the welfare of children

2   The Assessment Framework – guidance for social workers on undertaking assessments of children in need

3   Statutory Guidance on Learning and Improvement – arrangements for serious case reviews, reviews of child deaths and other learning.

Sport is named in the new guidance as having a responsibility to safeguard children. Staff, volunteers and contractors in sport, culture and leisure services have various degrees of contact with the children who use them, and appropriate arrangements will need to be in place. These should include:

• procedures for staff and others to report concerns that they may have about the children they meet that are in line with LSCB procedures

• appropriate codes of practice for staff, particularly sports coaches, such as those issued by governing bodies of sport, the Health and Safety Executive or local authorities.

*Working Together to Safeguard Children* (2015) can be downloaded via: www.sportscoachuk.org/inter-agency

The CPSU also has a briefing paper on the *Working Together to Safeguard Children* (2015) guidance, which can be downloaded via https://thecpsu.org.uk/news/2015/april/updated-guidance-for-people-working-with-children-in-england/

### What to Do If You're Worried a Child is Being Abused (2015)

This document provides best practice guidance for those who work with children in order to safeguard their welfare. It also contains an appendix to help

practitioners with the legal issues affecting the sharing of information.

The guidance also provides general information for anyone whose work brings them into contact with children and families, focusing particularly on those who work in social care, health, education and criminal justice services.

The document can be downloaded via: www.sportscoachuk.org/abuse-worry

### Local Safeguarding Children Boards

Every local area has an LSCB in place. LSCBs are multi-agency groups that coordinate local safeguarding activity and drive improvement to safeguard and promote the welfare of children more effectively. Many include safeguarding in sport subgroups to coordinate safeguarding across sport in the locality. Guidance on LSCBs can be downloaded via: www.sportscoachuk.org/LSCB

### Information Sharing

Sharing information is vital for early intervention to ensure children and young people receive the services they require. It is also essential to protect children and young people from suffering harm from abuse or neglect, and to prevent them offending. There has been confusion and uncertainty on the part of many professionals and volunteers working with children in all sectors about when, how and with whom concerns about the welfare or safety of children may be shared.

Following consultation, the government has developed and published guidance for immediate use by all practitioners who work with children or young people. *Information Sharing: Guidance for practitioners and managers* (2015) and the accompanying pocket guide provide the 'seven golden rules for information sharing':

1   Remember that the Data Protection Act is not a barrier to sharing information but provides a framework to ensure personal information about living persons is shared appropriately.

2   Be open and honest with the person (and/or their family where appropriate) from the outset about why, what, how and with whom information will, or could, be shared, and seek their agreement, unless it is unsafe or inappropriate to do so.

3   Seek advice if you are in any doubt, without disclosing the identity of the person, where possible.

4   Share with consent, where appropriate, and, where possible, respect the wishes of those who do not consent to share confidential information. You may still share information without consent if, in your judgement, that lack of consent can be overridden in the public interest. You will need to base your judgement on the facts of the case.

5   Consider safety and well-being – base your information-sharing decisions on considerations of the safety and well-being of the person and others who may be affected by their actions.

6   Necessary, proportionate, relevant, accurate, timely and secure – ensure the information you share is necessary for the purpose for which you are sharing it, shared only with those people who need to have it, accurate and up to date, shared in a timely fashion, and securely.

7   Keep a record of your decision and the reasons for it – whether it is to share information or not. If you decide to share, then record what you have shared, with whom and for what purpose.

More information can be found by downloading these guides: www.sportscoachuk.org/info-sharing

## Common Assessment Framework for Children and Young People

The Common Assessment Framework (CAF) is a key part of delivering front-line services that are integrated and focused around the needs of children and young people. The CAF is a standardised approach to conducting an assessment of a child's additional needs and deciding how those should be met. It can be used by practitioners across children's services in England.

The CAF promotes more effective, earlier identification of additional needs, particularly in universal services. It is intended to provide a simple process for a holistic assessment of a child's needs and strengths, taking account of the role of parents and environmental factors on their development. Practitioners will then be better placed to agree, with the child and family, what support is appropriate. The CAF also helps to improve integrated working by promoting coordinated service provision.

Further information on the CAF can be found via: www.sportscoachuk.org/CAF

## Protection of Freedoms Act 2012

From September 2012, there have been some changes to safeguarding arrangements in relation to vetting in England, Wales and Northern Ireland, arising from the Protection of Freedoms Act 2012. This includes a new and more limited definition of regulated activity. This new definition is intended to reduce the number and scope of positions that are eligible for a criminal records check with **barred list** information.

A new, more portable DBS online update service was introduced in England and Wales to allow individuals to apply for a criminal record certificate once, and then use this certificate when subsequently applying for similar posts (paid or unpaid).

## Multi-agency Safeguarding Hubs (MASH)

MASH have been established across England to receive and ensure a more coordinated response to referred concerns about children (and in some areas adults at risk) by a range of local statutory agencies.

## Safeguarding Children from Radicalisation

sports coach UK and the NSPCC have been working with the Police Counter Terrorism Unit following recent information suggesting that some adults who hold extremist ideologies and views have been using sports clubs as a method of targeting vulnerable individuals, in an attempt to influence their behaviour. The police have already begun work with sports coach UK and the NSPCC to minimise this risk through their 'Prevent' strategy, which deals with all forms of extremism. 'Prevent' is one of the four key areas of the Home Office's wider counter-terrorism strategy 'Contest' (consisting of 'Pursue', 'Prevent', 'Protect' and 'Prepare'). The aim is to prevent people from becoming radicalised by extremists before it happens. One aspect of the strategy is called 'Channel', which is a multi-agency approach to supporting people who are vulnerable to violent extremism. 'Prevent' aims to work with key partners, voluntary groups and communities to build resilience and capacity to deal with issues around extremism.

This programme works directly with the local community to safeguard communities that are at risk of being radicalised before radicalisation occurs. Unfortunately, it would appear that vulnerable young men, who have a variety of vulnerabilities, are at particular risk of being targeted by extremists.

Staff at the NCSPCC helpline and Childline are trained to provide advice, support and guidance for anyone concerned about radicalisation of young people.

More information on government anti-radicalisation strategy can be found here: www.gov.uk/government/publications/2010-to-2015-government-policy-counter-terrorism/2010-to-2015-government-policy-counter-terrorism

## Child Sexual Exploitation

The government defines child sexual exploitation as a form of child abuse. It occurs where anyone under the age of 18 is persuaded, coerced or forced into sexual activity in exchange for, amongst other things, money, drugs/alcohol, gifts, affection or status. Consent is irrelevant, even where a child may believe they are voluntarily engaging in sexual activity with the person who is exploiting them. Child sexual exploitation does not always involve physical contact and may occur online.

Many cases of child sexual exploitation have involved the sexual abuse and exploitation of large numbers of vulnerable young girls by (sometimes well organised) groups of (primarily) adult men or criminal gangs.

# Northern Ireland

Much of the legislation referenced in this resource can be mirrored to a degree of legislation in Northern Ireland based on the English and Welsh equivalent. Legislation and guidance are constantly changing, and this information is correct at the time of production (June 2016). For any further updates, please contact the CPSU in Northern Ireland on 028 90 351135.

## Children (NI) Order 1995

The Children (NI) Order 1995 is the **key** piece of legislation that deals with public and private law about children in Northern Ireland and is the equivalent in NI of the Children Act 1989 in England. It is based on five key principles:

- Paramountcy – the welfare of the child shall be the paramount consideration in any decision made.

- Parental responsibility – parents have responsibilities towards their children rather than rights over them. A wider range of people can now have parental responsibility.

- Prevention – preventing children from being abused and supporting them to promote their health and welfare.

- Partnership – the best way of meeting children's needs is to work with parents, and for agencies to work together.

- Protection – duty to investigate where a child is at risk of significant harm because of a lack of care or actual abuse.

More information is available via:
www.sportscoachuk.org/children-order

## Children Act 2004 in England and Wales

Only Section 1 of this Act deals with Northern Ireland, in relation to the role of the Children's Commissioner. Currently, this Act is not mirrored in Northern Ireland, but the Department of Health, Social Services and Public Safety (DHSSPS) introduced the Safeguarding Board (Northern Ireland) Act 2011 to enable them to launch the Safeguarding Board for Northern Ireland (SBNI).

The establishment of the SBNI strengthens inter-agency cooperation on child protection through replacing the four Area Child Protection Committees. This ensures cooperation on child protection and safeguarding arrangements at the highest level within key organisations such as police, local government and other statutory and voluntary organisations. It has an independent chair and clear lines of accountability to the minister at the Department of Health (NI) (DoH).

## Cooperating to Safeguard Children and Young People in Northern Ireland 2016

This is similar to 'Working Together to Safeguard Children in England' and 'Working Together Under the Children Act 2004' in Wales. This DoH document provides child protection guidelines and outlines the roles and responsibilities of all agencies.

DoH (2016) www.dhsspsni.gov.uk/publications/co-operating-safeguard-children-and-young-people-northern-ireland

## Sexual Offences (NI) Order 2008

When the Sexual Offences Act 2003 was passed by Parliament, a number of new child sex offences included in it were not extended to Northern Ireland. The introduction of the NI Order was intended to ensure children in Northern Ireland receive the same protections as those in England and Wales. The Order has seen the creation of new offences and increased tariffs for those who harm children. Part 2 of the 2003 Act was implemented in Northern Ireland in 2003 and focused on the notification requirements and a range of civil orders for public protection. More information can be found via: www.sportscoachuk.org/sexual-offences-order

## Criminal Justice (NI) Order 2008

This legislation has created public protection sentences within an overall new sentencing framework for

Northern Ireland, which removes the right to automatic 50% remission for prisoners who receive a custodial sentence. Arguably the most significant of the public protection sentences is the new indeterminate sentence, which will effectively mean that the offenders who receive this sentence will have to satisfy new parole commissioners that their risk of causing serious harm has been reduced before they are released from prison to return to the community.

The new legislation also places the Public Protection Arrangements (PPANI) (article 49) on a statutory footing and provides for the courts to order the use of electronic tagging for offenders. www.publicprotectionni.com/

## Criminal Law Act (NI) 1967

This is Northern Ireland-specific legislation with no equivalent elsewhere in the UK. It outlines an individual's responsibility in reporting child abuse. It states:

*Anyone with direct knowledge or information about an arrestable offence is required to inform the police within a reasonable time. An arrestable offence may include the non-disclosure of serious cases of child abuse.*

## Rehabilitation of Offenders (Exceptions) (NI) Order 1979

Ordinarily, due to the Rehabilitation of Offenders (NI) Order 1978, an employer is entitled only to request an individual's unspent record. However, exceptions are made under this legislation, which lists the circumstances in which an employer may apply for a full criminal records disclosure.

## Police Act 1997

This introduced what is known as Part 5 of the Police Act, which was not initially implemented in Northern Ireland. The Northern Ireland Office has now enacted this piece of the legislation. It enables the Police Service of Northern Ireland to disclose what is termed 'soft intelligence' (ie non-conviction information) when they deem it appropriate, and introduced enhanced criminal records checks. This coincided with the establishment of AccessNI, the equivalent in disclosure terms to the DBS in England and Wales. Barring decisions are taken by DBS for Northern Ireland.

## AccessNI

This is broadly similar to the DBS or Disclosure Scotland and facilitates disclosure checks. The organisation was established by a joint programme between the Northern Ireland Office, DHSSPS, Department of Education, and the Police Service of Northern Ireland. It provides registered organisations with a central means of checking the suitability of an individual seeking work with children by accessing any information that might have a bearing on an individual's suitability. Its role is to complement each agency's own safeguarding measures, and all agencies entrusted with the care or training of children need to have robust recruitment and staff/volunteer selection procedures. For more information visit www.nidirect.gov.uk/accessni or tel: 0300 200 7888.

## Protection of Freedoms Act 2012

From September 2012, there have been some changes to safeguarding arrangements in relation to vetting in England, Wales and Northern Ireland, arising from the Protection of Freedoms Act 2012, which amends the Safeguarding Vulnerable Groups (NI) Order. This includes a new and more limited definition of regulated activity. This new definition is intended to reduce the number and scope of positions that are eligible for a criminal records check with **barred list** information.

By late 2016, a new portable disclosure service is due to be introduced in Northern Ireland to allow individuals to apply for a criminal record certificate once, and then use this certificate when subsequently applying for similar posts (paid or unpaid). This was already introduced in England and Wales so UK-wide governing bodies of sport may notice a change in the administration process.

## Roles and Responsibilities

### Police

- Prevent, detect and prosecute behaviour that contravenes the law.

- Make referrals to the local health and social care trust if involved with a child where there are child welfare concerns.

- Investigate criminal offences committed against children.

- Gather evidence – this may include interviewing the child and their parents.

- Power to take immediate protective action to safeguard children, consulting with social services.

- Share information and intelligence with other agencies where this is necessary to safeguard children.

- Manage risks posed by dangerous offenders.

### PSNI Central Referral Unit (CRU) and Public Protection Unit (PPU)

The method by which the police service hear about many concerns regarding children is from members of the public, Health and Social Care Trusts (HSCT), as well as other agencies. A regional Central Referral Unit (CRU) provides a consistent and robust approach to the management of these concerns, or referrals as they are known, relating to child safeguarding, as well as other forms of vulnerabilities. Staff within CRU will work closely with colleagues in social services and decide how best each concern is managed. This may result in assigning the referral to a Public Protection Unit (PPU), or other relevant district, department or branch within the police service, for investigation.

PPUs are aligned to the five Health and Social Care Trusts and are made up of four elements namely:

1   The Child Abuse Investigation Unit (CAIU), staffed by trained child abuse detectives

2   Vulnerable Adults Officer

3   Domestic Abuse Officers

4   Offender Managers.

This make-up therefore enhances the ability of the police service, working closely with colleagues within social services, to deal with a range of issues involving children at a local level, including the abuse of children within the family or by someone known to them (current or historical); missing children; children living with domestic violence; and better manage the risk around those who have sexually or violently offended against children.

www.publicprotectionni.com/

### Health and social care trusts

There is a statutory duty under the Children (NI) Order 1995 to safeguard and promote the welfare of the child. Where there is a risk that a child is in danger of abuse or serious neglect, social care trusts must always intervene to safeguard them. In other situations where a family needs support or additional services to help them cope, social services may be able to help or offer advice, or may ask another professional or a voluntary agency to help. The Trusts hold statutory authority for the investigation of child protection concern and the exercise of statutory function under the Children Order.

### Gateway teams

These are the first point of contact in Trusts if you have concerns about a child or family. They will treat all contacts as enquiries in the first instance. Enquiries can include requests for information, advice and concerns about a child or family. An enquiry is always completed first; it is an initial filtering system before a referral is taken. If you make contact by phone, the duty worker will seek some general information about you, the child or family and the nature of your concern. On the basis of this information, they will be able to judge whether or not the enquiry should be progressed to referral. It is also possible to seek help though the NSPCC's 24-hour helpline 0808 800 5000.

### Further Reading

DHSSPS (2003) *Protection of Children and Vulnerable Adults (NI) Order 2003 Information Notes 1–3.* Belfast: DHSSPS. (Available via: www.sportscoachuk.org/ protection-children-order)

Volunteer Now (2011) *Getting It Right.* Belfast: Volunteer Now. (Available via: www.sportscoachuk.org/ getting-it-right)

Volunteer Now (2011) *Our Duty to Care.* Belfast: Volunteer Now. (Available via: www.sportscoachuk.org/ our-duty-to-care)

## Scotland

Many of the national guidance documents relating to safeguarding children are of interest and relevance in Scotland. The principles underpinning these documents also apply in Scotland. Every home country should be aware of, and respond to, the findings of any inquiries into the death of, or significant harm caused to, a child, regardless of where they live. However, responsibility for the care, welfare and protection of Scotland's children and young people is devolved to the Scottish Parliament. The Scottish Government therefore leads on issuing national policy, guidance and legislation that reflect national and local structures and the Scottish legal system, which includes the Children's Hearings System.

## Vision for Scotland's Children

The Scottish Government has agreed a vision for Scotland's children that provides the overarching context for the development of policy. The aim is that all children in Scotland are given every opportunity to develop to their full potential to become confident, responsible and productive members of society. The vision, embedded within the Children and Young People (Scotland) Act 2014, is that Scotland's children (up to 18 years old) should be:

- safe
- healthy
- achieving
- nurtured
- active
- respected
- responsible
- included.

These indicators are often referred to by the acronym SHANARRI.

## Getting It Right for Every Child

Getting It Right for Every Child (GIRFEC) is the Scottish Government's programme for children's services. It is an approach that puts children and young people at the centre of services and makes them a key part of finding solutions to their needs. Safeguarding and protecting children is therefore a significant part of the bigger picture.

The programme states that every child:

- deserves the best possible start in life
- deserves the same opportunities
- should get the help they need when they need it.

Scottish Government (2012) *Getting It Right for Children and Families*. Edinburgh: Scottish Government. ISBN: 978-1-780454-73-3. (Available via: www.sportscoachuk.org/right-for-children)

## National Guidance for Child Protection in Scotland (2014)

This guidance was updated in May 2014 and provides the current guidance and a national framework for anyone who could face child protection issues at work. Further guidance has been published for health

professionals, and protecting disabled children. Child protection committees will have their own inter-agency child protection procedures which are based on the national guidance.

NSPCC: www.nspcc.org.uk/preventing-abuse/child-protection-system/scotland/legislation-policy-guidance/

### For more info on named person see below:

www.gov.scot/Topics/People/Young-People/gettingitright/named-person

## Children's Hearings System

The Children's Hearings System is the legal system for children and young people in Scotland who are either at risk or have been caught offending. It seeks in the first instance to address children's 'needs not deeds'.

Children and their parents become involved in the Children's Hearings System if the child is getting into trouble with the police, there are concerns that they are being abused, they are taking drugs or alcohol, or they are not attending school. The Children's Hearings System makes decisions on what to do to help children, protect them and address their behaviour.

For more information on the Children's Hearings System and the Children's Hearings (Scotland) Act 2011, visit: www.childrens-hearings.co.uk

## Children (Scotland) Act 1995

This act provides the legislative framework for Scotland's child protection system. This defines adults as being over 16 years. It sets out:

- parental responsibilities and rights
- duties and powers public authorities have to support children and intervene if there are concerns about a child.

## Child Protection

Since 2000, when Scottish Ministers ordered an audit and review of child protection across Scotland, many steps have been taken, with the aim of improving services for children in Scotland through the Child Protection Reform Programme. Some of the outcomes of this programme include the following:

---

[43] Scottish Executive (2004) *Protecting Children and Young People: Framework for Standards.* Edinburgh: Scottish Executive. ISBN: 978-0755940-87-5. (Available via: www.sportscoachuk.org/protecting-children-framework)

- *Protecting Children and Young People: Framework for Standards*[43] – this set out what each child in Scotland could expect from professionals and agencies to ensure they are adequately protected and their needs met

- a children's charter[44] setting out what children and young people could expect to help keep them safe from harm

- guidance on the composition, role and responsibilities of Child Protection Committees

- a system of multi-disciplinary inspections of agencies providing services for children and young people

- an Integrated Assessment Framework designed to adopt a multi-agency approach to the assessment of children who are in need or who may require care and protection

- legislation, including the Protection of Children (Scotland) Act 2003, intended to improve the safeguards available for the recruitment and selection of staff and volunteers who work with children and young people; has now been replaced by the Protection of Vulnerable Groups (Scotland) Act 2007

- a public awareness campaign

- action to improve the range and quality of training available.

> *Child protection is the responsibility of all who work with children and families, regardless of whether that work brings them into direct contact with children. All workers should be fully informed of the impact of adult behaviour on children and of their responsibilities in respect of keeping children safe. Social work services and the police have a legal responsibility to investigate child protection concerns; they can only do this if they are made aware of those concerns.*
>
> **National Guidance for Child Protection in Scotland**[45]

The National Guidance is available via: www.sportscoachuk.org/scotland-child-protection

## Protection of Vulnerable Groups Scheme

The most recent change in legislation is the implementation of the Protection of Vulnerable Groups (Scotland) Act.

### Background

- The Protection of Vulnerable Groups (Scotland) Act 2007 (the PVG Scheme) has been live since February 2011.

- The scheme evolves from and builds on some of the existing provisions of the Protection of Children (Scotland) Act 2003.

- This law applies to organisations and groups across the statutory, voluntary and private sectors that provide services and activities for children, young people and/or protected adults. This includes Scottish governing bodies of sport (SGBs), sports clubs and other sports organisations.

- For the majority of SGBs, sports clubs and sports organisations, the PVG Scheme will relate to their work with children and young people. Only in very specific circumstances will it involve work with protected adults.

### Eligibility to join the scheme

- People doing regulated work with children, young people and/or protected adults can apply to join the PVG Scheme (eg sports coaches).

- On first application for membership of the scheme, checks will be carried out by Disclosure Scotland and a scheme record established for that individual. Unless these checks uncover information that makes the applicant unsuitable for regulated work with one or both of the above groups, the applicant will become a scheme member.

- It will be an **offence** for someone who is barred from regulated work to do, or seek to do, that type of regulated work. It will be an **offence** for an organisation to employ an individual in regulated work if that person is barred. The way to avoid either offence is to incorporate scheme membership into the recruitment process.

Further information about the PVG Scheme is available via: www.sportscoachuk.org/pvg-scheme

[44] Scottish Executive (2004) *Protecting Children and Young People: The Charter*. Edinburgh: Scottish Executive. (Available via: www.sportscoachuk.org/protecting-children-charter)

[45] Scottish Government (2014) *National Guidance for Child Protection in Scotland*. Edinburgh: Scottish Government. ISBN: 978-0-755997-79-4.

## Local Child Protection Committees (CPCs)

CPCs are the key inter-agency strategic vehicles for child protection work in each local authority. The voluntary sector, including sport and leisure, should be represented on each CPC. What is expected of a CPC is set out in *Protecting Children and Young People: Child Protection Committees*[46].

## Children's Services (Scotland) Bill

The Children's Services (Scotland) Bill 2007 is intended to support the reform of children's services. The outcome of this legislation is likely to be a duty on agencies to promote the well-being of children and to work together. The Bill also proposes measures to ensure the views of children are taken into account, and changes to the grounds for referring a child to the Children's Hearings System.

For more information on child protection in Scotland, visit: www.sportscoachuk.org/child-protection-scotland

or contact:

### Safeguarding in Sport
CHILDREN 1ST
61 Sussex Street
Glasgow G41 1DY
Tel: 0141-418 5674
Email: safeguardinginsport@children1st.org.uk
Web: www.safeguardinginsport.org.uk

To download Safeguarding in Sport's *10 Steps to Safeguard Children in Sport*, go to the website and click on the '10 Steps' button.

# Wales

## Children and Young People: Rights to Action

Published by the Welsh Assembly Government in 2004, *Children and Young People: Rights to Action*[47] is the Welsh equivalent of ECM. The strategy sets out the future direction of policy relating to children and young people and also how the Welsh Assembly Government intended to implement provision in the Children Act 2004.

Section 25 (2) of the Children Act 2004 sets out five core aims for safeguarding and promoting the welfare of children and young people in Wales:

- being healthy
- staying safe
- enjoying and achieving
- making a positive contribution
- achieving economic well-being.

In Wales, these five outcomes are also embodied in the Welsh Assembly Government's seven Core Aims, which are based on the United Nations Convention on the Rights of the Child. The aims are to ensure that all children and young people in Wales:

1   have a flying start

2   have a comprehensive range of education and learning opportunities

3   enjoy the best possible health and are free from abuse, victimisation and exploitation

4   have access to play, leisure, sporting and cultural activities

5   are listened to, treated with respect, and have their race and cultural identity recognised

6   have a safe home and community that supports physical and emotional well-being

7   are not disadvantaged by poverty.

Aim 4, relating to all children and young people having access to play, leisure, sporting and cultural activities has a section within *Rights to Action* and is further discussed in the Welsh Assembly Government's sport strategy *Climbing Higher*.

## Safeguarding Children: Working Together under the Children Act 2004

*Safeguarding Children: Working Together under the Children Act 2004*[48] is a key guidance document for all organisations providing services for, or working with, children and young people and is the main reference for safeguarding in Wales.

---

[46] Scottish Executive (2005) *Protecting Children and Young People: Child Protection Committees*. Edinburgh: Scottish Executive. ISBN: 978-0-755944-2-93. (Available via: www.sportscoachuk.org/protection-committees)

[47] Welsh Assembly Government (2004) *Children and Young People: Rights to Action*. Cardiff: Welsh Assembly Government. ISBN: 0-750498-76-5. (Available via: www.sportscoachuk.org/rights-to-action)

[48] Welsh Assembly Government (2006) *Safeguarding Children: Working Together under the Children Act 2004*. Cardiff: Welsh Assembly Government. ISBN: 0-750489-10-3.

The guidance sets out how all agencies and professionals should work together to promote children's welfare and protect them from harm. This includes organisations that are responsible for commissioning or providing services to children, young people and adults who are carers. It is intended to enable them to review their current policies, procedures and practices, analyse the current state of safeguarding and promoting children's welfare within their bodies and decide what steps are necessary in order to implement the guidance.

The guidance is available via:
www.sportscoachuk.org/children-act

## Local Safeguarding Children Boards

Since October 2006, each local authority area has operated an LSCB, which replaced the Area Child Protection Committees (ACPCs). The guidance for the development of LSCBs is contained within *Safeguarding Children: Working Together under the Children Act 2004.*

However, the Social Services and Well-being (Wales) Act 2014 (see below) introduces new regional safeguarding children boards to coordinate, and ensure the effectiveness of, work to protect and promote the welfare of children. Each regional board includes any local authority, chief officer of police, Local Health Board, NHS trust and provider of probation services that falls within the safeguarding board area. The regional boards are responsible for local child protection policy, procedure and guidance.

## Social Services and Well-being (Wales) Act 2014

The Social Services and Well-being (Wales) Act 2014 came into force in April 2016 it provided Wales with its own framework for social services.

The guiding principles of the Act include:

* giving individuals a stronger voice and more control over the care and support they receive

* encouraging a renewed focus on prevention and early intervention.

Provisions in the Act include:

* strengthening powers for safeguarding children and vulnerable adults

* establishing eligibility criteria which assess children and families on need rather than just on what services are available locally

* introducing a National Outcomes Framework for setting out what children and families can expect from social services

* introducing portable assessments, so that people who move from one part of Wales to another will receive the services they need in their new area

* introducing equivalent rights for carers so that they receive the same levels of support as the people they care for

* establishing a national adoption service.

The Act outlines how new regional safeguarding children boards coordinate, and ensure the effectiveness of, work to protect and promote the welfare of children. Each regional board includes any: local authority, chief officer of police, Local Health Board, NHS trust and provider of probation services that falls within the safeguarding board area. The regional boards are responsible for local child protection policy, procedure and guidance.

## Well-being of Future Generations (Wales) Act 2015

Puts in place seven well-being goals for everyone living in Wales.

1. A prosperous Wales
2. A resilient Wales
3. A healthier Wales
4. A more equal Wales
5. A Wales of cohesive communities
6. A Wales of vibrant culture and thriving Welsh language
7. A globally responsible Wales.

Each public body listed in the Act must work to improve the economic, social, environmental and cultural well-being of Wales. To do this they must set and publish well-being objectives.

These objectives will show how each public body will work to achieve the vision for Wales set out in the well-being goals. Public bodies must then take action to make sure they meet the objectives they set.

## Information Sharing

Sharing information is vital for early intervention, to ensure children and young people receive the services they require. It is also essential to protect children and young people from suffering harm from abuse or neglect, and prevent them from offending. There has been confusion and uncertainty on the part of many professionals and volunteers working with children in all sectors about when, how and with whom concerns about the welfare or safety of children may be shared.

The final chapter of *Safeguarding Children: Working Together under the Children Act 2004* is dedicated to information sharing, including reference to key principles and the legal background to information sharing.

## All Wales Child Protection Procedures[49]

This document contains guidance on roles and responsibilities for reporting concerns about a child's welfare or safety and addresses a wide range of safeguarding issues, including different mediums in which abuse can occur. The procedures outline the framework for determining how individual child protection referrals, actions and plans are made and carried out. They are based on the principle that the protection of children from harm is the responsibility of all individuals and agencies working with children and families, and with adults who may pose a risk to children. Partnership working and communication between agencies is identified as key in order to identify vulnerable children and help keep them safe from harm and abuse.

The procedures can be accessed via:
www.sportscoachuk.org/all-wales

## A Framework for Safeguarding and Protecting Children in and through Sport in Wales[50]

All children and young people in Wales have a right to experience sport and physical activity in a safe environment at whatever level they participate and in every setting. To promote safeguarding in sport, the *Framework for Safeguarding Children in and through Sport in Wales* was launched by Jane Hutt AM, the then Minister for Children, Education, Lifelong Learning and Skills, in 2009. The Framework has been developed in order to safeguard and protect children and young people in sport. It is based on current good practice and

informed by legislation, guidance and evidence from research, drawing from the fields of safeguarding and sport.

The Framework is available via:
www.sportscoachuk.org/wales-framework

## Protection of Freedoms Act 2012

From September 2012, there have been some changes to safeguarding arrangements in relation to vetting in England, Wales and Northern Ireland, arising from the Protection of Freedoms Act 2012. This includes a new and more limited definition of regulated activity. This new definition is intended to reduce the number and scope of positions that are eligible for a criminal records check with **barred list** information.

During 2013, a new portable disclosure service is due to be introduced in England and Wales to allow individuals to apply for a criminal record certificate once, and then use this certificate when subsequently applying for similar posts (paid or unpaid). This is due to be introduced in Northern Ireland from sometime in 2014 so UK-wide governing bodies of sport may notice a change in the administration process.

## CPSU Guidance: Duty of Care

It is widely accepted that, in relation to children and young people, sports clubs have a duty of care. The purpose of this section is to clarify what that duty entails and to provide some guidance as to what steps can be taken in order to demonstrate that this duty is being met. In essence, duty of care means that a sports club needs to take such measures as are reasonable in the circumstances to ensure individuals will be safe in using the activity to which they are invited or to which the activity is **permitted**.

A duty of care may be imposed by common law or statute, by contract or by acceptance by an individual. In some cases, the law imposes a duty of care (ie the duty of care the police have when they arrest someone).

There is no general duty of care upon members of the public towards the public at large. If, however, there is a formal relationship (eg between a club and a club member or a coach and an athlete), there is a duty of care.

[49] Welsh Assembly Government (2008) *All Wales Child Protection Procedures*. Cardiff: Welsh Assembly Government.

[50] CPSU/Sports Council for Wales (2009) *A Framework for Safeguarding and Protecting Children in and through Sport in Wales*. Cardiff: CPSU/Sports Council for Wales.

When children and young people are involved in organised sports activities and are, to any extent, under the care and/or control of one or more adults, the adults have a duty to take reasonable care to ensure their safety and welfare.

**The duty occurs in two ways:**

- a **legal** duty of care
- a **moral** duty of care.

The legal duty of care has a strict definition, and the most obvious example of this is in health and safety procedures. Clear guidance is provided as to what reasonable steps should be taken to minimise the hazards related to activities, substances or situations.

In many sports activities, given the health and safety considerations, it is recognised that a sports club owes a duty of care to its members. However, it is also understood and recognised that accidents can and do happen, and it is not possible to predict every eventuality. Liability for the **legal duty of care** would only arise when an incident occurs and it can be demonstrated that the risk was foreseeable, but no action had been taken to remedy it. In any subsequent legal action, the courts would apply the following criteria to determine if an organisation or individual would be held responsible:

- reasonable foreseeability of injury
- proximity
- fair, just and reasonable to impose a duty.

The claimant would have to show that:

- they were owed a duty of care
- the defendant breached this duty
- they suffered damage as a result of the breach.

It is recognised that there is a higher duty of care owed to children and young people and that this is something that those working with children and young people must recognise. An example of this is the Occupier's Liability Act 1957. This requires that an occupier must be prepared for children to be less careful than adults would be in a similar situation.

This will be even more so if the child is known to have learning difficulties or a medical condition that may make them more vulnerable than average to foreseeable risk of harm.

## Children and Young People in a Club

Any person in charge of children and young people involved in a sports club has a duty of care and should take all reasonable care for their safety. The duty when involved in a sports club is reasonably straightforward: it is comparable to the duty of a teacher in charge of a class of children of the same age. There have been many cases concerning liability for accidents suffered by school pupils while at school that can be usefully applied to the sports setting. Out of these cases has evolved a general principle that identifies the expected standard of care for teachers as that of a reasonably prudent parent, taking into account the fact that a teacher will have responsibility for a whole class of children.

This means that teachers are not required to achieve perfection with regard to their supervision of children, but that if they fall below the standards of a reasonably prudent parent, and injury is suffered as a result, the teacher may be held to be negligent. Those responsible for the management or supervision of children and young people in a club setting should consider what steps they may need to take in order to demonstrate the reasonable standard of care. Examples of this could include:

- keeping up to date registers of attendance
- keeping up to date records of contact details
- maintaining appropriate supervision ratios
- maintaining up to date information on specific medical conditions (eg allergies, asthma and epilepsy).

The Management of Health and Safety Regulations 1999 require that employers must make risk assessments and specify controls to reduce the risks of their activities. Those responsible for sports activities should consider themselves in a similar position to an employer and carry out a risk assessment for their activities. When carrying out risk assessments, it is vital to attend to the requirements relating to the duty of care and the other aspects of health and safety. Some sports have developed risk assessment templates, and it is important, if these have been developed, to complete them. It is not necessary to complete an assessment on each individual activity or session if it occurs on a regular basis. An annual or seasonal assessment would be sufficient. However, if hazardous equipment is used as part of the activity, this must be checked before the start of each and every session.

The **moral duty of care** is more correctly a **responsibility** for safety and welfare. Members of staff have a responsibility for those children and young people, and staff that are under their control.

To determine if a breach of the duty of care has occurred, the ordinary civil law of negligence would be applied. The question is whether the accused, in acting or omitting to act, has failed to reach the standard of a reasonable person. In specialist sports activities, the qualified instructor is responsible for the duty of care to all those taking part, irrespective of their age or position. The key point here is that the individual administering the activity, whatever their status, should be appropriately trained and authorised.

In addition to this, those in charge of children have an additional charge, and that is to act in loco parentis. This term is best explained as requiring the adult to act as 'a reasonable parent'. You will note that the adult is not necessarily the actual parent, but what the child's parent may permit, the sport may not. While a parent may say their child can stay out until midnight, a reasonable parent might not.

Within a sports club, fulfilling the duty of care would mean the responsible adult starts by ensuring the activity is authorised and the relevant instructors are qualified for the task, and would go on to ensure it is managed in a safe manner throughout.

## Reasonable Measures

This is best explained as what is considered to be reasonable. For sport, the CPSU has established the 'Standards for Safeguarding and Protecting Children in Sport'[51] to identify what an organisation should reasonably undertake in relation to child protection.

The standards (revised in 2016) require sports organisations (governing bodies of sport, CSPs and other support/national bodies) to have in place:

- a policy and procedure for responding to concerns (Standard 1)
- operating systems (Standard 2)
- measures for prevention (Standard 3)
- codes of ethics and practice (Standard 4)
- equity policy and procedures (Standard 5)
- communication policy and procedures (Standard 6)
- education and training (Standard 7)
- access to advice and support (Standard 8)
- an implementation/monitoring plan (Standard 9)
- influencing (Standard 10 – for CSPs and strategic organisations only).

For affiliated clubs, it is reasonable to expect that the governing body or wider organisation's policy and procedures will be incorporated into the club constitution and adhered to.

Other steps that would be considered reasonable measures would include adherence to guidance, advice or directions provided by a sports body or other relevant body. Many sports have developed guidance in relation to travel arrangements, recruitment and selection procedures, as well as training and qualifications, for example. For more information on guidance, please contact the relevant governing body.

The briefing paper this text was adapted from, and others, can be found on the CPSU website: www.thecpsu.org.uk

---

[51] CPSU (2016) 'Standards for Safeguarding and Protecting Children in Sport'. Leicester: NSPCC National Training Centre. (Available via: www.sportscoachuk.org/spc-standards)

# Code of Practice for Sports Coaches

## Rights/Relationships/Responsibilities

Coaches play a crucial role in the development of any sport and in the lives of the young athletes they coach. Good coaches ensure participants in sport have positive experiences and are therefore more likely to continue in their sport and achieve their potential.

Coaching, as an emerging profession, must demonstrate a high degree of honesty, integrity and competence at all levels. The need for coaches to understand and act upon their responsibilities is of critical importance to sport, as is the need to protect the key concept of participation for fun and enjoyment as well as achievement. This is implicit within good coaching practice and promotes a professional image of the good practitioner. This *Code of Practice* defines all that is best in good coaching practice.

## Good coaching practice needs to reflect the following key principles:

- **Rights**
  Coaches must respect and champion the rights of every individual to participate in sport.

- **Relationships**
  Coaches must develop a relationship with participants (and others) based on openness, honesty, mutual trust and respect.

- **Responsibilities – personal standards**
  Coaches must demonstrate proper personal behaviour and conduct at all times.

- **Responsibilities – professional standards**
  To maximise the benefits and minimise the risks to participants, coaches must attain a high level of competence through qualifications, and a commitment to ongoing training that ensures safe and correct practice.

| Principle | Statement | Issues | Actions |
|---|---|---|---|
| Rights | Coaches must respect and champion the rights of every individual to participate in sport | Coaches should:<br>• assist in the creation of an environment where every individual has the opportunity to participate in a sport or activity of their choice<br>• create and maintain an environment free of fear and harassment<br>• recognise the rights of all participants to be treated as individuals<br>• recognise the rights of participants to confer with other coaches and experts<br>• promote the concept of a balanced lifestyle, supporting the well-being of the participant both in and out of the sport. | • Treat all individuals in sport with respect at all times.<br>• Do not discriminate on the grounds of gender, marital status, race, colour, disability, sexual identity, age, occupation, religious beliefs or political opinion.<br>• Do not condone or allow any form of discrimination to go unchallenged.<br>• Do not publicly criticise or engage in demeaning descriptions of others.<br>• Be discreet in any conversations about participants, coaches or any other individuals.<br>• Communicate with and provide feedback to participants in a manner that reflects respect and care. |

| Principle | Statement | Issues | Actions |
|---|---|---|---|
| Relationships | Coaches must develop a relationship with participants (and others) based on openness, honesty, mutual trust and respect | Coaches:<br><br>• must not engage in behaviour that constitutes any form of abuse (physical, sexual, emotional, neglect, bullying)<br><br>• should promote the welfare and best interests of their participants<br><br>• must avoid sexual intimacy with participants, either while coaching them or in the period of time immediately following the end of the coaching relationship<br><br>• must take action if they have a concern about the behaviour of an adult towards a child<br><br>• should empower participants to be responsible for their own decisions<br><br>• should clarify the nature of the coaching services being offered to participants<br><br>• should communicate and cooperate with other organisations and individuals in the best interests of participants. | • Be aware of the physical needs of participants, especially the developmental stage and needs of children and young people, and ensure that training loads and intensities are appropriate.<br><br>• Ensure that physical contact is appropriate and necessary, and is carried out within recommended guidelines (provided by governing bodies of sport) with the participant's full consent and approval.<br><br>• Do not engage in any form of sexually related contact with any participant for whom you have responsibility. This is strictly forbidden as is sexual innuendo, flirting or inappropriate gestures and terms. Coaches are in a position of power and trust in relation to participants. By entering into an intimate/sexual relationship with a participant, a coach may be deemed guilty of abusing this position and, in relation to children and young people, this may also be unlawful.<br><br>• Inform parents or guardians immediately if you are at all concerned about the welfare of a child, unless there are concerns that this would not be in the interests of the child.<br><br>• Know and understand the relevant governing body of sport or employer child protection/safeguarding policies and procedures in this regard and adhere to them.<br><br>• Follow the reporting procedures laid down by your governing body of sport or employer if you have a concern – non-action is unacceptable.<br><br>• Arrange to transfer a participant to another coach if it is clear that an inappropriate or intimate relationship is developing.<br><br>• Discuss with parents and other interested parties the potential impact of the programme on the participant.<br><br>• Respect participants' opinions when making decisions about their participation in their sport.<br><br>• Encourage participants to take responsibility for their own development and actions.<br><br>• Allow participants to discuss and participate in the decision-making process.<br><br>• Discuss and agree with participants what information is confidential.<br><br>• Inform participants or their parents/guardians of the requirements of the sport.<br><br>• Inform participants or their parents/guardians of any potential costs involved in accessing the coaching services on offer.<br><br>• Be aware of and communicate on any conflict of interest as soon as it becomes apparent.<br><br>• Do not work with any other coach's participant without first discussing or agreeing it with both the coach and the participant involved.<br><br>• Identify and agree with participants which other experts or organisations could offer appropriate services. |

| Principle | Statement | Issues | Actions |
|---|---|---|---|
| Responsibilities – personal standards | Coaches must demonstrate proper personal behaviour and conduct at all times | Coaches:<br>• must be fair, honest and considerate to participants and others in their sport<br>• should project an image of health, cleanliness and functional efficiency<br>• must be positive role models for participants at all times. | • Operate within the rules and the spirit of your sport.<br>• Educate participants on issues relating to the use of performance-enhancing drugs in sport and cooperate fully with UK Sport and governing bodies of sport policies.<br>• Maintain the same level of interest and support when a participant is sick or injured.<br>• Display high standards in use of language, manner, punctuality, preparation and presentation.<br>• Encourage participants to display the same qualities.<br>• Do not smoke, drink alcohol or use recreational drugs before or while coaching. This reflects a negative image and could compromise the safety of your participants.<br>• Display control, respect, dignity and professionalism to all involved in your sport. |

| Principle | Statement | Issues | Actions |
|---|---|---|---|
| Responsibilities – professional standards | To maximise the benefits and minimise the risks to participants, coaches must attain a high level of competence through qualifications, and a commitment to ongoing training that ensures safe and correct practice | Coaches will:<br>• ensure the environment is as safe as possible, taking into account and minimising possible risks<br>• promote the execution of safe and correct practice<br>• be professional and accept responsibility for their actions<br>• make a commitment to providing a quality service to their participants<br>• actively promote the positive benefits to society of participation in sport, including the positive contribution sport can make to achieving improved outcomes for children and young people<br>• contribute to the development of coaching as a profession by exchanging knowledge and ideas with others, and by working in partnership with other agencies and professionals<br>• gain governing bodies of sport coaching qualifications appropriate to the level at which they coach. | • Follow the guidelines of your governing body of sport or employer.<br>• Plan all sessions so they meet the needs of the participants and are progressive and appropriate.<br>• Maintain appropriate records of your participants.<br>• Recognise and accept when it is appropriate to refer a participant to another coach or specialist.<br>• Seek to achieve the highest level of qualification available.<br>• Demonstrate commitment to continuing personal development (CPD) by undertaking/attending learning opportunities to maintain up to date knowledge of technical developments in your sport.<br>• Undertake/attend CPD opportunities to maintain up to date knowledge and understanding of other issues that might impact on both you and your participants.<br>• Be aware of the social issues and how your sport can contribute to local, regional or national initiatives.<br>• Actively participate in recruitment and education opportunities in your sport.<br>• Actively contribute to local, regional and national initiatives to improve the standards and quality of coaching both in your sport and sport in general.<br>• Practise in an open and transparent fashion that encourages other coaches to contribute to or learn from your knowledge and experience.<br>• Engage in self-analysis and reflection to identify your professional needs.<br>• Seek CPD opportunities to develop your coaching skills and competencies, and update your knowledge.<br>• Manage your lifestyle and coaching commitments to avoid burnout that might impair your performance.<br>• Do not assume responsibility for any role for which you are not qualified or prepared.<br>• Do not misrepresent your level of qualification.<br>• Promote good coaching practice in others and challenge any poor practice that you become aware of. |

## Implementation Issues

It is recognised and identified by the Ethics Review Group that a code of practice in isolation is of minimal value. In order for this code to fully impact on coaching practice and behaviour, it must:

- be incorporated into governing bodies of sport or employer constitutions and governance documents

- be a constituent part of a policy and procedure for dealing with allegations and complaints

- be used as the definitive guide and benchmark measure of coaching practice in determining any need for sanctions against a coach

- be fully incorporated into the coach education processes

- be assessed as part of the coach accreditation process

- be supported by the appropriate training and resources.

sports coach UK has developed a suite of training resources that underpin many of the concepts contained within this *Code of Practice for Sports Coaches*.

These include:

- *Safeguarding and Protecting Children* (formerly *Good Practice and Child Protection*)

- *Equity in Your Coaching*.

This *Code of Practice*, developed by sports coach UK, provides a guide for good and safe coaching practice.

sports coach UK will support a governing body of sport in implementing this code of practice.

sports coach UK will ensure that it has professional and ethical values and that all its practices are inclusive and equitable.

## Handout 1 – The Coach's Questionnaire

On reflection, how often in the last month did you:

• encourage a participant to input into the training session/programme

frequently/often/occasionally/rarely/never

• encourage a participant to make their own decisions about some aspect of training/competition

frequently/often/occasionally/rarely/never

• amend your session/programme as a result of input from a participant

frequently/often/occasionally/rarely/never

• make specific time to discuss progress with a participant

frequently/often/occasionally/rarely/never

• amend the coaching programme as a result of a participant's personal commitments outside sport

frequently/often/occasionally/rarely/never

• take time to discuss non-sport issues with a participant (eg about school, home)

frequently/often/occasionally/rarely/never

• demonstrate respect for, and interest in, a participant

frequently/often/occasionally/rarely/never

• ignore a participant's attempt to input into the session/programme

frequently/often/occasionally/rarely/never

• publicly chastise or severely criticise a participant

frequently/often/occasionally/rarely/never

• overrule the views of a participant

frequently/often/occasionally/rarely/never

• make a decision on behalf of a participant?

frequently/often/occasionally/rarely/never

## Handout 2 - The Participant's Questionnaire

On reflection, in the last month, did your coach:

- give you attention

  not at all/hardly ever/occasionally/often/a great deal

- give you an opportunity to make your own decisions

  not at all/hardly ever/occasionally/often/a great deal

- establish a good atmosphere in training

  not at all/hardly ever/occasionally/often/a great deal

- spend time discussing goals and priorities

  not at all/hardly ever/occasionally/often/a great deal

- encourage you to take responsibility for yourself

  not at all/hardly ever/occasionally/often/a great deal

- positively receive your ideas and act on them

  not at all/hardly ever/occasionally/often/a great deal

- take an interest in your life outside sport?

  not at all/hardly ever/occasionally/often/a great deal

On reflection, in the last month, how often did you feel:

- like giving up your sport

  not at all/hardly ever/occasionally/often/a great deal

- disenchanted with training/your sport

  not at all/hardly ever/occasionally/often/a great deal

- valued by the coach

  not at all/hardly ever/occasionally/often/a great deal

- highly committed to your training and sport?

  not at all/hardly ever/occasionally/often/a great deal

## Handout 3 - Is it Acceptable?

You may wish to ask yourself the following questions and, if the answer is *yes*, try to establish in what circumstances they apply. Does the age of the participant make any difference to your answers?

Is it ever acceptable to:

- push a participant so hard, they are regularly reduced to tears

- ridicule a participant publicly

- undermine a participant's feelings of self-worth

- ignore or disregard a participant repeatedly

- have a sexual relationship with your participant

- meet with your participant regularly on their own

- provide physical support for your participant (ie handle them)

- take a participant alone to your home

- enter a participant's bedroom

- transport one participant regularly on their own in your car

- raise concerns if you feel the behaviour of another adult towards their participant is unacceptable

- report the behaviour of another adult (eg coach, official, parent) to a senior person, the police or social services?

© Alan Edwards

# Handout 4 - Signs of Child Abuse

## Neglect

| Physical Signs | Behavioural Signs |
|---|---|
| The child: | The child: |
| • is constantly hungry | • is tired all the time |
| • is in an unkempt state; frequently dirty or smelly | • frequently misses school or is late |
| • is losing weight or constantly underweight | • fails to keep hospital or medical appointments |
| • is dressed inappropriately for the weather conditions | • is left alone or unsupervised on a regular basis |
| • has untreated medical conditions – is not being taken for medical treatment of illness or injuries. | • has few friends |
|  | • is a compulsive stealer or scavenger, especially of food. |

## Physical Abuse

| Physical Signs | Behavioural Signs |
|---|---|
| The child has: | The child: |
| • injuries they cannot explain, or explain unconvincingly | • is reluctant to have parents contacted |
| • injuries that have not been treated, or have been treated inadequately | • has aggressive behaviour or severe temper outbursts |
| • injuries on parts of the body where accidental injury is unlikely, such as the cheeks, chest or thighs | • runs away or shows fear of going home |
| • bruising that reflects hand or finger marks | • flinches when approached or touched |
| • cigarette burns or human bite marks | • is reluctant to get changed for PE or school sport |
| • broken bones (particularly if they are under the age of two) | • covers up their arms and legs with a long-sleeved shirt, even when it is hot |
| • scalds, especially those with upward splash marks, tidemarks on arms, legs or on the body (caused from standing in hot water). | • shows signs of depression or moods that are out of character with their general behaviour |
|  | • is unnaturally compliant to parents. |

## Sexual Abuse

| Physical Signs | Behavioural Signs |
|---|---|
| The child has: | The child: |
| • pain, itching, bruising or bleeding in the genital or anal area | • shows sudden or unexplained changes in behaviour |
| • any sexually transmitted disease | • makes sexual drawings or uses sexual language |
| • recurrent genital discharge or urinary tract infections, without apparent cause | • has an apparent fear of someone |
| | • possesses unexplained amounts of money or receives expensive presents |
| | • runs away from home |
| | • takes a parental role at home and functions beyond their age level |
| | • has nightmares or wets the bed |
| | • is not allowed to have friends (particularly in adolescence) |
| | • is self-harming, self-mutilating or has attempted suicide |
| | • alludes to secrets they cannot reveal |
| | • is reluctant to get changed for PE or school sport |
| | • displays sexualised behaviour or knowledge (particularly in young children) |
| | • has eating problems, such as anorexia or bulimia |
| | • abuses drugs or other substances. |

## Emotional Abuse

| Physical Signs | Behavioural Signs |
|---|---|
| The child: | The child: |
| • fails to grow or thrive (particularly if they are thriving away from home, eg on trips or at matches) | • has compulsive nervous behaviour, such as hair-twisting or rocking |
| • suddenly develops speech disorders | • is excessively deferent towards others, especially adults |
| • has delayed physical or emotional development. | • is unwilling or unable to play |
| | • shows an excessive lack of confidence |
| | • has an excessive fear of making mistakes |
| | • shows an excessive need for approval, attention and affection |
| | • self-harms or self-mutilates, or attempts suicide |
| | • shows an inability to cope with praise |
| | • is reluctant to have parents contacted. |

## Handout 5 – What Action Would You Take?

Identify what action you would take in each of the following scenarios:

1  You are Simone's coach. Simone is 14 years old and confides in you:

   *My stepdad got into my bed last night when my mum was on night duty. He said he could not sleep because he was cold. He said he was just getting to know me better, and I should not tell Mum as she would not believe me. He said I would be put into a home if I told her. I'm scared and don't know what to do. I don't want to tell anyone, especially not my mum. She took an overdose when her last boyfriend left.*

2  You are a coach at the local club and work alongside Tom when coaching the junior squad. You and Tom have known each other for over 10 years and are great friends. Carla, one of the 13-year-old players from the squad, asks to speak to you and confides:

   *Can I talk to you? I'm scared and don't know what to do. Tom gives me a lift home in his car from coaching each week. Last night, he tried to kiss and cuddle me. He told me not to tell, that it would be our secret and that I was someone special and really talented, and I'd be thrown out of the club if I told anyone. You won't say anything, will you?*

3  You are Jane's coach. Jane is 14 and confides in you:

   *You must promise not to tell anyone, but I think I am pregnant. I'm really scared. My dad will kill me if he finds out. I feel like running away. I don't know what to do. Don't tell anyone, will you?'*

4  A new coach arrives in the area and has come along to your club to ask if there are any opportunities to coach there. The club has a recruitment policy, part of which requires that all new volunteers/coaches complete a self-disclosure form. The coach is a little hesitant but agrees to complete the form. On the form, he indicates that he has a conviction for unlawful sex with a minor, and possession of drugs. His references indicate that he is reliable and a very good coach. What do you do?

5  You have heard that the coach of the under-13s team has been showering with the players after training and matches. What do you do?

6  Within your role as welfare officer, you receive a letter of complaint from the parents of one of your female players, Joanna. The letter details a number of different incidents when the coach has sworn and shouted at Joanna for not training hard enough and talking when she was meant to be training. What would you do?

7  One of the coaches within the club asks to speak to you in confidence, in your capacity as welfare officer for the club. She explains that she has been watching Derek, one of the senior coaches in the club, and that she is uneasy about some of the methods he is using when coaching the under 13s. She explains that she has seen him make some of the young people do press-ups and run around the playing area, she believes, as punishments. She is very concerned and considers this inappropriate. What would you do?

8  You are the welfare officer at your club. You receive an anonymous letter telling you Sophie (one of your 15-year-old players) is seeing John (20 years old), who is one of your coaches. John is one of your star coaches who you have mentored for over two years. What would you do?

9  Your club's under-14 side has just won the league after playing in a nail-biting final against its long-standing rivals. After the match, you are all in the clubhouse, celebrating and awaiting the presentation of the trophies. Terry, coach to the winning team, has just bought the team a round of beers/lagers, and is encouraging the team to drink them in one. Terry has coached the team for the last two years and has been a coach at the club for 12 years, and a friend of yours for over 20 years. What do you do?

10  You are treasurer of the club, and one of the female players, Jenny, asks to speak to you in confidence about her brother Fred, who is one of the club's star players. Fred (aged 15) is very worried about coming to training, but realises that if he doesn't, then he will not be eligible for selection for the team for Saturday. Fred has told Jenny that Dave (the club chairman) tried to kiss him. Dave told Fred that if he told anyone, he would be dropped from the team and even banned from the club. What would you do?

# Need to know your role in the safeguarding and protection of children?

Child Protection in Sport Unit
**play sport** stay safe
**enjoy** and **achieve**

**NSPCC**

sports coach
**UK**

## Refreshers

**'Safeguarding and Protecting Children 2: Reflecting on Practice' (SPC2)**
*Reflect, learn and share safeguarding best practice*

If you have attended SPC1 and need to refresh your safeguarding training, this is the best workshop to attend, as it will do more than merely repeat the basic knowledge you learnt in SPC1. You'll reinforce and strengthen your understanding of safeguarding and share your thoughts with other coaches. Learn from their experiences to help you create a positive, child-centred sporting environment.

**OR**

**'Renewal: Safeguarding and Protecting Children in Sport'**
*You can now refresh and update your understanding of safeguarding at your convenience*

This online course enables you to update your understanding of safeguarding at a time to suit you. An alternative to attending a face-to-face workshop, this fantastic course can be completed at home – on a tablet or PC – so you can dip in and out to suit your lifestyle, while keeping track of your progress. It includes two modules that give you the chance to look at two important areas of safeguarding you might not have great awareness/experience of: Positive Sports Parent; and Safe Communication with Digital Kids.

To find out more about this eLearning, visit **sportscoachuk.org/safeguardingelearning**

eLearning

To attend SPC2 or complete the eLearning, you must have completed SPC1. It is not suitable if you have no previous safeguarding training or are under 18.

## First-time attendee options

**'Safeguarding and Protecting Children' (SPC1)**
*Create a positive sports experience for young people*

The SPC1 workshop will give you the best-practice tools you need to recognise and respond appropriately to issues of safeguarding and child protection. This will increase your confidence and help you create a positive sports experience for young people.

Attendees who have been on SPC 13+ can progress to SPC1, but not before they turn 16.

### Safeguarding Overview

There is nothing more important than the safety and protection of children. That's why there are workshops many governing bodies of sport regard as essential for coaches prior to them going out and coaching. They will assist you in carrying out your role safely and effectively. If you haven't been on a safeguarding and protecting children workshop, there are two options available to you.

Most governing bodies of sport recommend you refresh your safeguarding training at regular intervals (eg every three years)*.

>> **[13+]**

**'Keeping Safe in Sport: Safeguarding for Young Volunteers (13+)' (SPC 13+)**
*For young volunteers in sport between the ages of 13 and 17*

This workshop provides you with age-appropriate safeguarding information, helping you to identify how and when you should take action and how you can keep yourself safe in sport.

* Check with your governing body of sport for further information, and to ascertain whether or not attendance at safeguarding workshops is required before you commence coaching. Also check they recognise completing the eLearning as being an appropriate way to renew your safeguarding training.

125

# Our Vision

Putting coaching at the heart of sport.

# Our Mission

To drive the development of sports coaching in the UK.

# Strategic Objectives

To achieve our mission, we will:

1 champion and drive **policy and investment** in coaching

2 support and challenge our Partners to improve their **coaching systems** in order to achieve their objectives

3 provide **products and services** to support our Partners and their coaches

4 provide **research** and share **good practice** that will benefit coaching

5 ensure an effective UK coaching agency through quality **leadership**, good governance and a **skilled team**.

sports coach UK will ensure that it has professional and ethical values and that all its practices are inclusive and equitable.